POSITIVE POWER

POSITIVE POWER

31 Devotions To Help Unleash Your Positive Power

By
Eugenia Johnson-Smith

Copyright © 2023 by Eugenia Johnson-Smith
Cover copyright © 2023 by Positive Power, LLC

Lyles, Johnson and Smith Publishing supports the right to free expression and the value of copyright. The purpose of copyright is to encourage writers and artists to produce the creative works that enrich our culture. The scanning, uploading, and distribution of this book without permission is a theft of the author's intellectual property. If you would like permission to use material from the book (other than for review purposes), please contact EugeniaJohnsonSmithPP@gmail.com. Thank you for your support of the author's rights.

Positive Power
Lyles, Johnson and Smith Publishing
4086 Elora Lane Lexington, Kentucky 40515
PositivePowerllc.com
Facebook: Positive Power LLC

First Edition: December 2023
Positive Power is a division of Positive Power, LLC
The Positive Power name and logo are trademarks of Positive Power LLC
The publisher is not responsible for websites (or their content) that are not owned by the publisher.

To schedule a Positive Power speaking event go to: EugeniaJohnsonSmithPP@gmail.com.

Positive Power books may be purchased in bulk for business, educational, or promotional use.
For information, please contact EugeniaJohnsonSmithPP@gmail.com
Print book interior and cover design by Tom Monarch Graphics.

ISBN: 978-1-963264-00-5 (paperback),
ISBN: 978-1-963264-01-2 (ebook)

Printed in the United States of America

DEDICATION

I dedicate this book to my Lord and Savior who has given me the strength, courage, and Positive Power to let my light shine through the pages of this book. This is dedicated to my family who stood by me on my writing journey. For the many eyes that rolled just before they agreed to read another one of my stories or said, "Yes I'll listen," as I eagerly read to them. And specifically, to my husband, Stan, who has been a constant supporter and audience of one. To my mother in heaven, whose handwritten Notes:: of encouragement I always found when I needed them the most. To my dad, thank you for your support and for listening to me read one more story. To my sisters, what can I say? You guys have always had my back, held me up, and cheered me on every step of the way. You read, critiqued, and edited this devotion - on our first Sister Trip. That was truly the trip of a lifetime, and I will treasure it forever. To my niece and favorite school teacher, I appreciate your guidance.

To Neil Chethik, my teachers, and staff at the Carnegie Center, and to my mentors Mrs. Karen Leet, "my writer mom," and Ms. Claudia Love, "my soul sister" you guys are the best and I love you both so much. You two are my writing guides and took me under your wings, nurtured me, trained me, and helped me develop strong writing wings. There were times I soared like the eagle and there were times when the rejections came but I kept the faith. I knew my time would come and I leaned on Isaiah 40: 31 KJV "But they that wait upon the Lord shall renew their strength; they shall mount up with wings as eagles; they shall run, and not be weary, and they shall walk, and not faint." Now I am soaring with the eagles above the clouds.

I also dedicate my book to you the reader, because without you my words would go unread. It was written to let you know that you're not alone. You were in my thoughts as I placed the words on the pages. I wrote it for you.

I hope my words encourage and inspire you to unleash your Positive Power, and as you read and explore each chapter, more of your power is released.

ACKNOWLEDGMENTS

To my sorority sisters of Alpha Kappa Alpha Sorority, Inc. The Beta Gamma Omega Chapter, Lexington, Kentucky you have been there for me from the beginning and allowed me to share my Positive Power with you over the years.

Thank you to the Carnegie Center staff and teachers for all your love and support on my writing journey and for making me feel at home.

Thank you, Neil Chethik, for seeing something special in me and providing me the opportunity to grow and develop as a writer. You supported and encouraged me from day one, and always had your door open to me. And thank you for your vision of the Kentucky Black Writer's Collaborative. You're the best.

Karen Leet, what can I say a great big thanks for your friendship and mentorship and for taking me under your wings as my "Writer Mom." You were a friendly face at the beginning of my writing journey. You are a blessing.

Claudia Love Mair, I love your spirit. I thank you for your guidance, support, and all you do for the KBWC. You inspire me and I am grateful to have you as my writer sister and mentor.

You both have been my writing guides and took me under your wings, nurtured me, trained me, and helped me develop strong writing wings. There were times I soared like the eagle and there were times when the rejections came but I kept the faith. I knew my time would come and I leaned on Isaiah 40: 31 KJV "But they that wait upon the Lord shall renew their strength; they shall mount up with wings as eagles; they shall run, and not be weary, and they shall walk, and not faint." Now I am soaring with the eagles above the clouds.

Thank you to the Lexington Writer's Room for being a place where creativity can grow and flourish. You provided me with a community of writers, many of whom have helped me during this process.

To my Blah, Blah, Blah Writer's Group, thank you for providing a space for writers to meet, support each other, and grow as writers.

To my Beta Readers and Proof Readers, Pastor Weese, Rev. Veda Stewart, Pam Dorell, and Francene Botts, thank you for your time and your attention to detail.

Tom Monarch Graphics, without your expertise and assistance with the formatting this book. Thank you for helping to make my dream a reality.

WHAT PEOPLE ARE SAYING ABOUT POSITIVE POWER

"Positive Power offers a way forward for people of all ages who are struggling with doubts and insecurities and for those who are on the path to positive living. It is rooted in faith and amplified by heartfelt stories. The book is an encouragement to embrace the hard work of becoming the person we are meant to be. I especially value the questions that guide readers to deeper levels of engagement with themselves and their faith."

~Charisse L. Gillett, Ed.D, President, Lexington Theological Seminary

"Eugenia's engaging writing will move readers & change lives as she shares her own positive power with others! She's a real blessing and her uplifting stories can empower your life."

~Karen Leet Carnegie Center for Literacy and Learning

"Eugenia Johnson-Smith herself is a source of positive power and readers will resonate with the uplifting message in this, her first devotional. In a world in which we can all be made to feel powerless, Positive Power is exactly the right medicine to lift bent heads and straighten rounded shoulders. I heartily recommend this gentle guide."

~Claudia Love Mair, author of Mourning Pages (Broadleaf Books, 2024)

TABLE OF CONTENTS

Foreward..1
Introduction...2
Devotion One..5
Devotion Two...17
Devotion Three..25
Devotion Four..31
Devotion Five..38
Devotion Six..46
Devotion Seven.......................................53
Devotion Eight..60
Devotion Nine...70
Devotion Ten...78
Devotion Eleven......................................85
Devotion Twelve......................................94
Devotion Thirteen.................................104
Devotion Fourteen................................112
Devotion Fifteen...................................121
Devotion Sixteen...................................128
Devotion Seventeen..............................138
Devotion Eighteen.................................148
Devotion Nineteen.................................155
Devotion Twenty...................................162
Devotion Twenty-One...........................170
Devotion Twenty-Two...........................177
Devotion Twenty-Three........................182
Devotion Twenty-Four..........................189
Devotion Twenty-Five...........................195
Devotion Twenty-Six.............................202
Devotion Twenty-Seven........................209
Devotion Twenty-Eight.........................217
Devotion Twenty-Nine..........................224
Devotion Thirty......................................234
Devotion Thirty-One.............................242
Positive Prayer For You........................250

FOREWORD

Eugenia Johnson-Smith is one of the most positive people I have ever met in my life. That's why it's no surprise that her devotional messages exude that same joyful energy. It speaks to the heart, mind, and soul while employing simplistic and awe-inspiring meditations that help us to truly self-activate and actualize our power within. From healing exercises to practical journaling, it offers its readers a variety of ways to bring positivity into their day.

It allows us to tap into our own sense of power and engage interactively to transform our thoughts to improve our disposition and our position.

This book will be a blessing to all who open the pages and open their hearts to the positive power that lies within each of us. I know you will enjoy the journey and I am grateful to God that these words were written and will not return to the reader void but will fill our cup until it overflows.

From ideas in the atmosphere to the reality of pen to the paper, we have been waiting for this gift. We are grateful to the author and her willingness to share her words and unleash God's positive power into our lives.

Dr. Veda Stewart,
Embry Chapel AME Elizabethtown, Kentucky

INTRODUCTION

We all have the Positive Power inside us to do great and awesome things. It doesn't matter if you have never been told you can do anything, have been encouraged or not. You can do and achieve anything. You are destined for greatness. You have the power to succeed and to be anything you desire to be.

You have the power within to overcome any obstacle. If you feel you are all alone and no one sees you, you are not alone. People see you. There's a whole family of Positive Power People (P3s) here to support your dreams, visions, and goals. Here to cheer you on to the victory life has for you, here to show you love, and here to encourage you to listen to the power of your own voice - not the negativity of others.

This book will help you to overcome the "Ifs" in your life. "If I was smarter. If I had more time. If I could just..." What are the ifs you can't shake? Which ones are paralyzing you and stopping you from living your life without limits? You can renew your spirit with the power of each new day and begin to appreciate the little things each day has to offer.

Do you feel you have been stuck in the mud of life and can't move? Is there no one around to toss you a rope or offer you any help? You can find the power to let go, and the power to move on. You can find hope, healing, and forgiveness to help you pull yourself out of the stagnation you were stuck in for so long.

This book will help you connect to a positive power source that will never run out, run down, or run out on you. It will allow your inner light to shine bright, and it will give you the wings you need to soar over doubts, fears, and limiting beliefs so that you can fly to the moon of possibilities and beyond.

You will tap into your faith which will help you to find the inner peace you need to make the much-desired positive changes in your life.

This book will help you become like an eagle. Once you open your heart and mind you will have an eagle's eye view of your future. You will soar with grace over any mountain you encounter. When anything blocks your way, you can fly above it or change direction. Don't be afraid to take a detour or to pause for a much-needed rest-stop. You have the power to change the course of your life at any point along your journey.

You have the power to succeed at anything you do. The power lies in you with the help of your positive power source and the words you speak. Your words have power. This book will help you to unleash the positive power that has always been inside you.

I invite you to open your heart, mind, and spirit and go on this journey of transformation. Let me help you tap into your energy that is there just under the surface waiting to be released. Set it free.

Before we start I invite you to pray the Positive Power Prayer with me.

Dear Lord, I thank you for this day. I thank you for this moment of knowing that I am being thought of in a positive and loving way by others who are reading this at this exact moment. Amen. Every time you pray this prayer, you are connecting with others who are reading this book, praying this prayer, and are on this positive power journey of discovery with you.

You are not alone. We are all connected.

POSITIVE POWER

DEVOTION ONE

The Power of A Smile

*"Yet I will rejoice in the Lord,
I will joy in the God of my salvation."
Habakkuk 3:18 KJV*

A Smile

A smile, has the power to lift spirits.

A smile, has the power to change minds.

A smile, has the power to move mountains.

A smile, has the power to melt frozen hearts.

A smile, has the power to comfort the bereaved.

A smile, has the power to heal the hurt.

A smile, has the power to connect without saying a word.

A smile, has the power to break down barriers.

A smile, has the power to welcome the lost.

So go ahead, share your Smile.

Give it away.

It may be the only Smile they see today!

Eugenia Johnson-Smith

S   Salvation

M   Meditate on the Word of God

I   In Him All Things Are Possible

L   Love Unconditional

E   Everlasting Life

I'm a child of God therefore,
I always have something to SMILE about!

When you see someone smile doesn't it make you smile? Did you know smiles are contagious? When you smile at someone they will smile back. The positive energy you give off when you smile prompts others to smile. Try it today, pass your smile on to everyone you come in contact with.

Every morning and afternoon on my school post as a school crossing guard I smile and say good morning or have a good evening. It's important that I greet each child and parent with a smile because I could be the only bright spot in their

POSITIVE POWER

day. I have received cards at Christmas and at the end of the school year that express how much they appreciate seeing my smile each morning and how it makes their day. When I am not there, they miss my smile.

By connecting and spreading our smiles to others we are creating a more positive impact on our family, our community, and our world. Remember a smile is free yet powerful. A smile is a priceless gift that can be given even when we have nothing else to give and it's the only gift that it's okay to return. So go ahead share your smile. Give it away. It may be the only one they see today. Our smile could be a sign of caring that saves a life.

Don't feel like smiling? Are there days you can't find anything to smile about? Are there days that you are in so much pain you can't smile, or days you're so tired you just can't smile? Is today one of those days?

Smile anyway even if you must fake it. Genuine or fake both cause the brain to produce endorphins and serotonin which causes positive emotions. In addition, they can boost the immune system, reduce stress, and lower blood pressure.

Do you feel you don't have a reason to smile? For those who can't find a reason to smile or don't feel like smiling, I want to remind you that as Christians and children of God we always have a reason to smile.

Don't consider yourself a Christian. I invite you to read and decide this day to accept Christ as your Lord and Savior, or to renew your commitment to him.

"Be it known therefore unto you, that the salvation of God is sent unto the Gentiles and that they will hear it."
Acts 28:28 KJV

S – Salvation We are saved! The Bible gives us many reasons to smile.

"For God did not send His Son to condemn the world, but that the world through Him might be saved."
John 3:15 KJV

POSITIVE POWER

Even on our worst days, we can and should Smile. As Christians, we may have heard the phrase "trouble don't last always and joy comes in the morning." When we have those moments we should meditate on the fact that Jesus gave His life for us. And that should put a smile on our faces! Be Happy.

"Rejoice in the Lord always again I say, rejoice!"
Philippians 4:4 KJV

If we are blessed by God and He is our Savior, we will always have something to smile about, no matter what else is going on in our lives. We can all find something positive to smile about. Some folks are sad if they wake up and it's raining. I say, "Look at that beautiful rain. God is cleansing the earth of all of the dirt, filth, and impurities. His will be done." We have to be careful when we view the things of the world with our eyes and not surrender to God's will. We may not be able to understand God's logic, but we know that everything He does is good and perfect and has a purpose according to His will. That's something to smile about!

M – Meditate on God's Word.

Eugenia Johnson-Smith

"In the beginning was the Word and the Word was with God and the Word was God. He was in the beginning with God. All things that were made through Him, and without him, nothing was made that was made."
John 1:1 KJV

He made us so we are special to Him. He will take care of us and our needs. That should make us smile!

I – In Him all things are possible.

"I can do all things through Christ who strengthens me."
Philippians 4:13 KJV

When we know and believe in God, we can do anything we set our minds to do. That should also make us smile! Just think about the awesome power of doing all things, whatever things we can imagine. Wow! The list is infinite. That should make us smile!

POSITIVE POWER

L – Love God's Love is unconditional

"But God commendeth his love toward us, in that, while we were yet sinners, Christ died for us." Romans 5:8 KJV

We know that God loves us despite who we are and what we have done in our past. Even when no one else loves us, He loves us. Even when we don't love him, God loves us. Even when we don't love ourselves, God loves us. God loves us when we don't follow all of the commandments. We only need to repent and ask for forgiveness. Because of His grace and mercy, we will be forgiven. God Loves Me and He loves you too! That should make us smile.

E - Everlasting Life - *"For God so loved the world that he gave his only begotten Son that whosoever believed in him shall not perish but have everlasting life." John 3:16 KJV* Christ died for us, in our place for our sins. He died so we don't have to die the eternal death. If that is not enough to make you smile you are in big trouble!

Eugenia Johnson-Smith

"I love the man that can smile in trouble, that can gather strength from distress and grow brave by reflection."

Thomas Paine

POSITIVE POWER PRAYER

Dear Lord, I thank you for this day. I thank you for this moment of knowing that I am being thought of in a positive and loving way by others who are reading this at this exact moment. **Dear God, help me to remember that because I have you I will always have something to smile about. Help me to be willing to share my S.M.I.L.E with everyone I come in contact with.** *Amen.*

POSITIVE POWER STUDY

List three ways you share your Smile with others.

_____
_____
_____
_____
_____
_____
_____

Do you desire the kind of S.M.I.L.E. Jesus can give?

_____
_____
_____
_____
_____
_____
_____

If yes, I invite you to recommit or accept Christ this day as your Lord and Savior.

POSITIVE POWER

Pray this prayer of repentance or this prayer of renewed commitment.

I_____ a sinner, accept Jesus as my Lord and Savior on this day_____.
(Date)

I believe Jesus is the son of God and that he died for my sins and that he arose on the third day and ascended into heaven and that one day I will be with him. Amen.

I_____ renew my commitment to Jesus my Lord and Savior on this day_____.
(Date)

Lord, from time to time my commitment to you may have wavered, but you never left me. I renew my commitment to you and seek a closer relationship with you. Thank you for sticking with me. Amen.

Eugenia Johnson-Smith

Notes:

POSITIVE POWER

DEVOTION TWO

The Power of Appreciation

"Naked I came from my mother's womb, and naked shall I return there. The Lord giveth, and the Lord taketh away; Blessed be the name of the Lord!" Job 1:21 KJV

Why don't we appreciate what we have until it's gone? How many times have you heard that statement or even said it yourself?

Today I planned to wear a pair of recently purchased earrings. However, when I went to retrieve them from my pants pocket the place I put them that morning to my surprise, I only found one earring. I was crushed. I had only worn them once. I purchased them from a jewelry sale at a local hospital fundraiser.

I had complained a couple of times about how this year's selection was not as good as last year's and this vendor didn't offer the same selections. My disappointment was the result of going there with a particular item in mind. I wanted to purchase the exact same pair of earrings I had gotten the year before that I loved so much. They were three inter-linking mesh silver loops.

As you can guess they did not have the earrings I was hoping for. My entire attitude had taken a nosedive so anything I purchased was already doomed. I managed to see a different pair of earrings and thought they were cute so I purchased them. This pair was 2 smooth silver loops, not as fancy as the others.

Complaining not so much about the earrings, but about the process of getting the earrings still sent negative energy relating to the earrings – and now they were gone. At the moment of my loss, I was sad and I missed my earrings. I wanted my earrings. I loved my earrings. I valued my earrings. And I realized I now appreciated my new earrings as much as my first pair.

I retraced my steps in hopes of finding them. Walking and searching in the cold, eyes glued to the ground like a hound dog on a trail on the way to my car.

POSITIVE POWER

I looked through the elevator crack desperate to see a sparkle or glimpse of my earring yet hoping it really wasn't there, because if it was, what good would it do? How would I get it and who could I ask to get it for me? No, it wasn't there, so on with my search.

Arriving at my car I was at the end of my hunt. Still no earring. Not on the ground of the passenger side door, the back seat, or even in between the passenger seat and the floorboard. Oh well, it's gone. That's what I get for not appreciating them when I first purchased them.

So off I went back to where my journey had begun. Aha! A glimmer of hope. What if I left it at home and it was never in my pocket? What if it was never with me? The day went on and my mind was other places and there was no more thought of the lost, unappreciated earrings.

My day was done, errands and appointments had all been completed, and I was finally home. I got out of my car and looked down to see my beautiful sparkling earring. I was happy, excited, and in disbelief all at the same time. After an entire day of searching, I was blessed to have them back. Now most appreciated! Those who know me, know that I quickly picked up the earring and sanitized it so I could wear it the very next day.

This story was about a missing earring, but it's really not about the earring. Rather it's about the lack of appreciation we have for the things God has blessed us with, both materially and spiritually. Things like shelter, transportation, food, and family. Maybe we don't live in a mansion. But a 1-room apartment or a 3-bedroom home provides the shelter we need. Maybe we don't dine on the finest of gourmet meals. But we are fed. Maybe we are riding the bus because our car is broken down or we can't afford a car. Yet we are getting where we need to be. Maybe we don't appreciate our family members and friends because they are acting out or strung out on drugs. But just having those friends and family members with us is something to appreciate.

Some of us may have jobs that drive us crazy, with long hours and no pay increases. Here we go complaining. In an instant, it could all be gone. That's when we realize what we had was

POSITIVE POWER

not so bad after all. We wish we had it back, long hours and all.

Eugenia Johnson-Smith

POSITIVE POWER PRAYER

Dear Lord, I thank you for this day, I thank you for this moment of knowing that I am being thought of in a positive and loving way by others who are reading this at this exact moment. I ask you to grant me the Power of Appreciation, help me to be thankful for all blessings you have given me big and small. Help me to see that a blessing I see as small is big in your eyes. Lord help me to be grateful for all you have done for me and all you plan to do for me. Amen.

POSITIVE POWER STUDY

List 3 things in your life you appreciate and why you appreciate them.

1._____

2._____

3._____

Who or what do you take for granted?
_____
_____
_____
_____
_____
_____
_____

How do you show appreciation?
_____
_____
_____
_____

Eugenia Johnson-Smith

Notes:

POSITIVE POWER

DEVOTION THREE

The Power Of Being

"And be not conformed to this world: but be ye transformed by the renewing of your mind, that ye may prove what is that good, and acceptable, and perfect will of God." Romans 12:2 KJV

Being is the essence of who we are as a person, it is how we live and it is what makes up our core. We have the power to determine who we will become. We can change if we aren't happy with who we are or with who we are becoming.

Be Magnificent. Let your inner beauty shine and touch the hearts of others. Be Brave. Don't live within the boundaries others set. Live a limitless life. Be Curious. Dare to dream, and live your dreams!

Be Audacious. This is your time to step out in faith and do something outside the box. Be Unstoppable. Don't let anyone or anything stand in the way of achieving your goals, even if the person standing in the way is you.

Be Meek. But do not be a doormat. The meek shall inherit the earth. Be Sweet. Be a good person. Be a good friend, and be a person people can trust. Be Sassy. Do you! Be your unique one of a kind self. It's okay to be different. Different is Good! Be Smart. Be like a sponge and soak up all the knowledge you can from books and from the lessons life teaches you.

Be Kind. Treat people with dignity and respect no matter their station in life. Acknowledge that at any given moment it could be you in need. Show the same kindness to others that you would expect were the situation reversed. Be Committed to Love and to being loved.

Be Unsettled. Don't settle for mediocrity. Be Classy. Head held up, but not so far up that you look down your nose at others.

Be Inspiring. Let your life inspire others in thought, word, and deed. Let your thoughts direct your words and your words lead your actions.

Be Encouraging. Learn to recognize all opportunities to offer encouragement.

POSITIVE POWER

Acknowledge that it may come in different forms, a smile, a pat on the back, a hug, a text message, or a hand-written note. And yes even a phone call or even a personal visit. Be Helpful. Help others as you have been helped.

Be Happy. No one likes a *Grumpy Dump* or a *Party Poop*. Be Nice. Share a delightful and pleasant atmosphere with those around you. Be Respectful. This applies to you and to others in thoughts, words, and actions as it relates to the words you speak and the things you post on social media.

Eugenia Johnson-Smith

POSITIVE POWER PRAYER

Dear Lord, I thank you for this day, I thank you for this moment of knowing that I am being thought of in a positive and loving way by others who are reading this at this exact moment. Bless me with the Power of Being all I can be. Help me to know I am all these things and much more. Help me not to conform to the world but help me to change the world positively as I let my light shine for you. Amen.

POSITIVE POWER STUDY

What are the top 3 – 4 Bes you need to work on?

_____
_____
_____
_____

What are the top 3 – 4 Bes that work for you?

_____
_____
_____
_____

What Bes do you need to focus on in order to become the awesome person you are destined to Be?

_____
_____
_____
_____
_____
_____

Eugenia Johnson-Smith

Notes:

DEVOTION FOUR

The Power of Being Positive

Some people have the ability to see something positive in every situation. Even in the worst of situations, I can find something positive about it. Over the years I realized I have been blessed with the gift of positivity.

> *"Both riches and honor come from You, And you reign over all. In Your hand is power and might: In Your hand it is to make great And to give strength to all."*
> *1 Chronicles 29:12 ESV*

I believe in the power of God! I know He gives me power. He has blessed me with the ability to pass on that Positive Power to you by helping you tap into your very own positive power source. With that power, we have the ability to get ourselves out of any negative, harmful or hurtful situation. God is a God of peace, purpose, and love. He doesn't want us to hurt, fail or be in a negative place in our lives.

1 Chronicles 29:12 ESV and Luke 1:37 ESV are two very powerful verses. I feel the power as I read and meditate on the words. They tell us

Eugenia Johnson-Smith

that all we need comes from Him. If we need a financial blessing, He's got us. If our broken hearts need mending, He's got us. If we need to be comforted, He's got us. If we need healing, He's got us. If we need peace of mind, He's got us. He has power over all things. He is in control.

If at this very moment you find yourself in a situation where you feel powerless over it, believe with me that the God who created us did not make a mistake and everything He made is good. And because of that, you are destined for greatness. Greatness, I argue, is relative to you. You may not be great on the national stage like Oprah Winfrey, but you are great in the lives of those you've touched in a positive and powerful way. And to them, you are their "Oprah Winfrey". We must dig deep within ourselves to unleash the strength and power He has given us.

Being positive has helped me get through many difficult situations including the loss of my mother. She was and continues to be my biggest cheerleader from heaven. Her spirit of positivity flows through me and because of it, I can smile through my tears. Being positive helped me as I dealt with the news of cervical spine surgery. It was my positive power and that of my positive power people that I leaned on during my healing

POSITIVE POWER

process. It was painful, tearful, and uncomfortable at times but my ability to be positive through it made all the difference.

Me + God = Positive Power

Your Positive Power is activated when you add God to every situation. He is there just waiting for us to call on him in every situation, both good and bad. He was there with me at every stage as I faced cervical spine surgery. He got me through it.

"For nothing will be impossible with God."
Luke 1:37 ESV

Eugenia Johnson-Smith

POSITIVE POWER PRAYER

Dear Lord, I thank you for this day. I thank you for this moment of knowing that I am being thought of in a positive and loving way by others who are reading this at this exact moment. Help me to acknowledge the blessing of the Power of Being Positive. Help me to acknowledge that I have the power to be positive because I have the Power of God within me. Amen.

POSITIVE POWER STUDY

Do you consider yourself to be a positive person? Why or why not?
_____
_____
_____
_____
_____

List 3 Positive Things about yourself.
1)_____
2)_____
3)_____

How do you feel?
_____

What or who is your positive power source?
_____
_____
_____

Whose life have you touched in a positive way?
_____
_____
_____
_____
_____

Eugenia Johnson-Smith

What negative influences do you need to eliminate from your life?

___

In what ways can you be more positive?

___

POSITIVE POWER

Notes:

Eugenia Johnson-Smith

DEVOTION FIVE

The Power of Being Thankful

"In everything give thanks: for this is the will of God in Christ Jesus concerning you."1 Thessalonians 5:18 KJV

Are you the "Glass Half-Full" or "Glass Half-Empty" type of person? Half-full people see life like this, "Thank You Lord for what I have. I only have to work a little harder and my glass will be full." They focus on the blessings they have, not on what they don't have or on what they can't do. Having overcome many challenges to get them to where they are today, they know they have made it this far. They know they have made it halfway and if they keep pressing on they will make it to the very end. The prize!

What is your glass half full of? Possibilities? Hopes? Dreams? What puts "cracks" in your glass? Fear? Doubt? Shame? All of these "cracks" in your glass allow your possibilities, hopes, and dreams to fall out and be lost. These are the negative thoughts that stop your half-full glass from becoming a tall, full glass of endless

POSITIVE POWER

possibilities! If that is where you are, it's time to stop up the holes.

Time to stop fear, stop doubt, stop shame. It's also time to stop procrastinating, and to stop excuses to allow our glasses to be filled with all God has for us. When we are thankful for the smallest things, we appreciate them for the wonderful blessings they are. We value them as precious gifts from God, It's important that we express it with a thankful heart. This shows we don't take any blessing for granted. He will bless us abundantly.

When we live with a thankful heart, every day will be thanksgiving. Not the turkey day, but a day we wake up grateful for a glass overflowing and grateful for the hope of Each New Day!

When we live each day being thankful, everything looks better and brighter. Our old dented beat-up car doesn't look so bad when we pass a car sitting on the side of the road, with one of those bright colored stickers on the window indicating that it's been there for a while.

Eugenia Johnson-Smith

"Give thanks to the Lord, for he is good: his love endures forever."
Psalm 118:1 NIV

I'm thankful for Jesus Christ, my Savior, who suffered bled, and died on the Cross so that a sinner such as me would have the opportunity through his grace and mercy to have an everlasting life. I'm so truly thankful for that. It puts a smile on my face every day. I don't have all the riches of the world. I'm okay because I have the gift of eternal life and that can't be taken away, lost, or stolen.

Do we say, "thank you" when someone does something for us? Don't only text or email. Why not pick up the phone and say, "thank you?" Then, take it to the next level and take the time to send an "old-fashioned" hand-written "thank you" note. It is becoming a lost art. I love receiving handwritten Notes::. Pre-printed thank you cards are fine as well. Why not start with those? Find one that fits your personality or the situation.

POSITIVE POWER PRAYER

Dear Lord, I thank you for this day, I thank you for this moment of knowing that I am being thought of in a positive and loving way by others who are reading this at this exact moment. Help me to be thankful for all you do and have done for me. Help me to express my thanks to those you have put in my life to love and care for me. I am thankful to have you in my life. Amen.

POSITIVE POWER STUDY

What do you want out of life?

_____
_____
_____
_____
_____

Share an incident you are thankful for that helped you get to this moment?

_____
_____
_____
_____
_____

How are you becoming more thankful for where you are today?

_____
_____
_____
_____
_____
_____
_____

POSITIVE POWER

Why do you see your glass as half full or half empty?

_____
_____
_____

List three things you are thankful for:

1._____
_____
_____
_____
_____

2._____
_____
_____
_____
_____

3._____
_____
_____
_____
_____

Which represents your life? Half full or half empty? Why?

_____
_____
_____
_____
_____
_____
_____
_____

Share your list with someone. By sharing your list you are empowering others with *The Power of Being Thankful.*

POSITIVE POWER

Notes:

Eugenia Johnson-Smith

DEVOTION SIX

The Power Of Connection

"So we being many, are one body in Christ, and every one members one of another."
Romans 12:5 KJV

God created us and everything that is was created by Him, therefore we all are connected.

"In the beginning, God created the heaven and the earth."
Genesis 1:1 KJV

From the first man, Adam, and the first woman, Eve, all other men and women were born. We all are brothers and sisters, and a spiritual connection flows through each of us. It was in us even before we were born.

"So God created man in his own image, in the image of God created he him; male and female created he them."
Genesis 1:27 KJV

Have you ever thought of someone and at that moment the person called you on the phone or

POSITIVE POWER

just stopped by for a visit? Or have you gotten a feeling in the pit of your stomach just before receiving bad news? You felt something was wrong with your child or sibling. That's the power of connection. We all have it. Some of us are more open to it than others. Some pass the feelings off and fail to make the connection.

Because of our connection, we are spiritually responsive to the needs of others. God has placed us on earth to care for and work with each other. He has provided the world with all the natural resources we need to live. He has blessed us with the talents, skills, and knowledge to create any other needed resources. Our common thread of creation produced a forever spiritual connection uniting each of us and it can never be broken. Our connection may become weak, it may be forgotten, and it may even get lost. But it will never break. It is unbreakable!

The power of connection is especially strong during a natural disaster. Communities and the nation come together in prayer, come together to provide supplies and come together to rebuild. In these situations our differences are invisible and our power of connection is strong, remembered, and found. It is never broken. *"For as we have many members in one body, and all members have not the same office;..."*

Romans 12:4 KJV

Social media can give you a false sense of connection. You may have hundreds of likes and Facebook friends and a strong Instagram following. Yet, you may feel alone and forgotten. You are not alone, you just need to be reminded of your power of connection to God, family, friends, and total strangers. As you reach out to others through personal contact, your power of connection will start to become stronger. You will no longer feel alone or isolated. You will be reconnected.

POSITIVE POWER PRAYER

Dear Lord, I thank you for this day, I thank you for this moment of knowing that I am being thought of in a positive and loving way by others who are reading this at this exact moment. I open myself up to the power of connection so that I will no longer feel alone or isolated. Help me to connect to others so that I can relieve their feelings of isolation. Amen.

Eugenia Johnson-Smith

POSITIVE POWER STUDY

When do you feel most connected to others?

List instances when you have thought about someone just before they called or visited.

How would you describe your sense of connection?

POSITIVE POWER

Describe an incident that can only be explained as a spiritual connection.

Eugenia Johnson-Smith

Notes:

POSITIVE POWER

DEVOTION SEVEN

The Power Of Direction

"In all thy ways acknowledge him, and he shall direct your paths."
Proverbs 3:6 KJV

"Thy word is a lamp unto my feet, and a light unto my path."
Psalms 119:105 KJV

You may know your destination. You may know the mode of travel you will take to get there. How soon you get there depends on the direction you choose. Below are examples of three different directions that will get you to the same destination:

Example A – **The Straight Route:** This route goes straight through the center of town. It has lots of traffic lights and lots of traffic.

Example B - **The By-Pass:** This route is longer in terms of miles but has no traffic lights and a higher speed limit that compensates for the extra miles.

Example C – **The Scenic Route:** This route is the longest of them all and a bit out of the way.

It offers views of beautiful rolling hills, stone fences, and Thoroughbred Horses frolicking in the fields.

The direction you choose to take may depend on many different circumstances. If time is not an issue, you may select The Scenic Route for a relaxing casual drive. If time is a concern you may select either the Straight Route or The By-Pass to get you to your destination. The final decision between the two depends on other factors, such as time of day or night, day of the week, or activities in the downtown area. The Straight Route may be quicker at night or during off-peak traffic times, thus making it the right direction to go for your particular journey.

When selecting the direction you wish to go, it is important to remember that you are in control of the route you take. It is perfectly okay to start out going one direction and to change directions in the midst of your trip or even to start over. You just need to know when it's time to make the change.

Are you currently doing the same things the same way you always have done them? Have you ever considered that there could be a better or more efficient way of doing things? Have you ever been new to a city and only known one way to get to work or the mall? In your world, it's the

POSITIVE POWER

only direction that will get you there. Your friend picks you up to go to the mall and off you go in another direction. Wow! The new way was so much faster and gave you much more time to shop.

In life, don't you want to spend more time at the destination than you do getting there? Is it time to change the focus of where your life is going? Don't be afraid to try new directions. There are many paths that can lead you to the same location. Some can get you there faster while others may take you longer but will give you great experiences. Still, others will set you off on an entirely new path.

It reminds me of the night we drove to my sister's house for Thanksgiving. The GPS instructed us to stay in the right lane as we took the exit. We did as directed but ended up on the original road. We repeated this process at least two more times before my niece said, "Go straight." We laughed so hard we cried. We were stuck in an endless loop going in the same direction. We needed a slight directional change to get us back on track.

The Power of Direction is in your hands. You have control. Which path will you take?

Eugenia Johnson-Smith

POSITIVE POWER PRAYER

Dear Lord, I thank you for this day, I thank you for this moment of knowing that I am being thought of in a positive and loving way by others who are reading this at this exact moment. I also thank you for the Power Of Direction. I ask that you grant me the wisdom to know the right direction to take for my journey. Amen.

POSITIVE POWER STUDY

What direction are you heading in regard to your life goals?

_____
_____
_____
_____
_____

a) your career?

_____
_____
_____
_____

b) your education?

_____
_____
_____
_____

c) your relationship?

_____
_____
_____
_____
_____

Where has your current direction led you?

_____
_____
_____
_____
_____
_____
_____
_____
_____
_____
_____
_____
_____
_____
_____
_____

When will it be time for you to change directions?

_____
_____
_____
_____
_____
_____
_____
_____

POSITIVE POWER

Notes:

Eugenia Johnson-Smith

DEVOTION EIGHT

The Power Of Each New Day

"Whereas you do not know what will happen tomorrow. For what is your life? It is even a vapor that appears for a little time and then vanishes away."
James 4:14 NKJV

Each New Day truly is a blessing from God. I thank Him for it early in the morning. If it were not for today, all that I am would be what I was when I laid down to sleep last night. But when my eyes opened up this glorious morning, I was given the gift of today, to right the wrongs of yesterday, and to have another opportunity to fulfill my hopes and dreams. As long as we have life, we are not defeated. We can still learn and grow and improve on our masterpiece of life. As long as we have breath, the "fat lady" cannot sing.

So, say Good Morning to Each New Day with Enthusiasm and Wonder! This is just to say hi and wish you the best as you start your day. Each new day is a new beginning, a chance to

POSITIVE POWER

do better than you did yesterday, a chance to do more than you did yesterday, and a chance to start with a clean slate. We can't change what is in the past. But we can make improvements here in the present so that the future will be better. Each new day is one day closer to our goals.

No matter how hard we try, we can never change the past. No matter how much we may want to. We can only act on the present and we are not guaranteed a future. Many people living in this moment will not have the next.

Would you do things differently if you knew this was your last moment? Would you treat people differently knowing this was your last moment? Would you pay more attention to things you take for granted or view as insignificant if you knew this was your last moment?

I say live today as if it is your last day! Do not live carelessly and recklessly. But savor every moment. Savor every breath. Savor every vision as if it is the last time you will see a sunset or sunrise, hear a bird chirp, smell a flower, or see someone you love.

If you knew this was your last day, would you care that you got cut off in traffic? Would you care that you were in the 20 items or less line and the person in front of you had a minimum of 50 items? Would you care that no one noticed you had on a new suit or dress? Would it even matter?

Flip side, someone got up this morning to find that her child didn't wake up. Flip side, someone got the results that his test said stage four cancer. Flip side, someone got word that her husband was killed in the war. Flip side, someone's house was foreclosed on and now he is homeless.

What if the "Flip Side" was your tomorrow? Would you spend more time with your child encouraging him and showing him how much you love him? Would you take care of the only body you have, making sure to eat right, exercise, and get the proper amount of sleep each night? Would you nag your husband, wife, or significant other less and thank God more for the blessing of a loving companion in your life? Would you be a better steward of your money, managing your finances more responsibly?

POSITIVE POWER

Each New Day is not always about righting the wrongs we have done to others; it's also about righting the wrongs we have done to ourselves. It's about the missed opportunities caused by our bad choices, bad decisions, indecisiveness, fear, or lack of knowledge. Today let us forgive our past missed steps so we can boldly step into our future.

"Therefore I say unto you, what things soever ye desire, when ye pray, believe that ye receive them, and ye shall have them."
Mark 11:24 KJV

God has blessed us with life and as long as we have life, we have hope. We have opportunities. We have the means to accomplish our hearts' desires. We just need to tap into that place where we acknowledge that we cannot change the past. The place where we acknowledge we can only learn from it, and accept it as the past and move on. Dwelling on it will not change it. That is the place where we acknowledge that today truly is a gift from God! That is the place where we acknowledge that tomorrow is not promised; and if today really is our last day, that it was a Good day!

Eugenia Johnson-Smith

Let us not focus on yesterday or tomorrow, but let us focus on making today the best day of our lives. We must embrace the new day we are blessed with. It allows for a new beginning, a fresh start or a rebirth. It's an ability to rewrite the story of our lives and a chance to flip yesterday's script.

"...If God be for us, who can be against us?"
Romans 8:31 KJV

"No weapons that is formed against thee shall prosper..."
Isaiah 54:17 KJV

If we are blessed to wake up, we have been given another chance. Don't blow it! This could be our last.

New running shoes $95, new Hybrid vehicle $25,000, Each New Day Priceless!

POSITIVE POWER PRAYER

Dear Lord, I thank you for this day. I thank you for this moment of knowing that I am being thought of in a positive and loving way by others who are reading this at this exact moment. I thank you for the blessing of Each New Day. Help me not to waste it by dwelling on things I don't have and help me not to spend it worrying about things I can't change or control. For I know that You hold all Power in Your hands. I know when I put my faith in You there is no need to worry. For You are an awesome and all wise God and I will commit Each New Day to you. Amen.

POSITIVE POWER STUDY

What do you need to let go of today so you can receive the gift of a new day?

_____
_____
_____
_____
_____

What or who are you taking for granted?

_____
_____
_____
_____
_____

What are your hopes and dreams that a new day will offer you?

_____
_____
_____
_____
_____
_____
_____

POSITIVE POWER

What would you do differently if you knew this was your last day?

___

...your last week?

___

...your last month?

___

...or your last year?

Eugenia Johnson-Smith

List three things you can do to make today one of the best days of the rest of your life.

POSITIVE POWER

Notes:

Eugenia Johnson-Smith

DEVOTION NINE

The Power of Encouragement

"Have not I commanded thee? Be strong and of a good courage; be not afraid, neither be thou dismayed; for the Lord thy God is with thee wheresoever thou goest."
Joshua 1:9 KJV

No matter what you may be going through, sickness, heartbreak, loss of a job, or divorce, you are not alone. You are not the first to experience these things, nor will you be the last. I know these words don't take away the pain and suffering you are feeling, but God's word can.

When we are feeling weak and we can't go any further, that's when we need to be reminded that God is there to help us along the way. He is there to pick us up when we fall and to heal our wounds. He has the power that will heal the brokenhearted and comfort those who grieve.

"Let not your heart be troubled; ye believe in God, believe also in me."
John 14:1 KJV

POSITIVE POWER

You may be dealing with those who seek to destroy you physically, spiritually, or emotionally. Often, we find it frustrating to deal with these situations and find the only way to handle them is on our knees. There will be times in your life when you can't fight the battles you face alone. You must turn it over to the Lord.

> *"For the Lord Your God is he that goeth with you, to fight for you against your enemies, to save you."*
> *Deuteronomy 20:4 KJV*

> *"There hath no temptation taken you but such as is common to man: but God is faithful, who will not suffer you to be tempted above that ye are able; but will with the temptation also make a way to escape, that ye may be able to bear it." 1 Corinthians 10:13 KJV*

Are you battling an addiction, or are you being tempted by the desires of the flesh? You are not alone in these situations. God is still here and He is here for you. He will not put more on you than you can handle. It may seem hard and hopeless, but you can kick the addiction and resist the desires with the Power of God. There will be stumbling blocks you will have to face and navigate around. Some will be placed in your path by others and some will be placed in your path by you. At times your journey may not be easy and you may want to quit. Don't give up. Keep the faith. The journey may be long and lonely, but it is not impossible.

Following my spinal surgery I had difficulty finding a comfortable pillow. I made several purchases but, I could not get any relief. Sleep was impossible. I was in tears from lack of sleep. I needed some serious Positive Power.

It was time for me to drink from the positive power well. I called on my three sisters for support and encouragement. They were ready to pour into me during my time of need. They reminded me that God was here, too. He's never left us. He has always walked beside us and carried us when we needed a lift. Sometimes we need a gentle reminder.

I eventually found a comfortable pillow and got the rest I needed.

POSITIVE POWER

"But Jesus beheld them, and said unto them, With men this is impossible; but with God all things are possible."
Matthew 19:26 KJV

Even though there will be many times when you need encouragement, there will also be opportunities for you to encourage others. Your power to encourage others will come from your very own testimony, of how you were able to face and overcome the difficulties and hardships of your life. Even when you go through your darkest times, you gain the power to light the way for others who may be on a similar journey.

The words that encourage me are, I can do all things with Christ. These words fill me with power, courage and hope and the knowledge that I am not alone. It doesn't matter the situation I know with Christ I will get through it according to his will and you can, too.

Eugenia Johnson-Smith

POSITIVE POWER PRAYER

Dear Lord, I thank you for this day. I thank you for this moment of knowing that I am being thought of in a positive and loving way by others who are reading this at this exact moment. I thank you for the Power of Encouragement to face my temptations and to lean on your words and not my own understanding. I'm encouraged that I don't have to fight my battles alone anymore. Amen.

POSITIVE POWER STUDY

Who's in your corner?

Who are your cheerleaders?

Eugenia Johnson-Smith

List times when you need to be encouraged.

_____
_____
_____
_____
_____
_____
_____
_____
_____
_____

List ways you encourage others?

_____
_____
_____
_____
_____
_____
_____
_____
_____
_____
_____

POSITIVE POWER

Notes:

Eugenia Johnson-Smith

DEVOTION TEN

The Power Of Forgiveness

"So when they continued asking him, he lifted up himself, and said unto them, "He that is without sin among you, let him first cast a stone at her."
John 8:7 KJV

Mistakes, seen or unseen, heard or unheard, all have made them. Some of us pretend we haven't and most of us hardly ever or rarely mention our mistakes. Yet we can find time to point out the mistakes of others. Many go to extremes to make sure they are heard and now with the help of social media will make sure those mistakes are seen and known.

What makes us want to know every little gory or sleazy detail about the mistakes of others while at the same time seeking to do everything in our power and beyond to keep ours hidden? Do we secretly think we are better than others? Or is it, that in our case, it was just as they say? "I didn't

POSITIVE POWER

do it intentionally." No, I don't think we are better than anyone else. But when it's us, our family, our friends, or even our favorite celebrity, it's hard to believe that people we know, love, and idolize could be capable of making a mistake like that.

We're all created in the image and likeness of God. According to the US Constitution/Bill Of Rights, we are all granted equal rights and the pursuit of happiness. Yet, for some, we feel we can sit in judgment. "No, that's not me," you're thinking. Well ponder this for a moment, have you ever said something like this? I would never do that..., I couldn't do that..., or I don't see how they let that happen..., or I would never allow myself to be put in that situation. Guess what? You're judging.

We must not fall victim to our mistakes. They shouldn't and don't define who we are as long as we acknowledge them and when needed pay our debt to society. We use them as life lessons to learn from and to help others avoid the same mistakes we made. That's how we help ourselves and each other.

Everyone makes mistakes and nobody's perfect. There will be times when we'll make a mistake and have to ask forgiveness. And there will be times when others will ask forgiveness of us. We must be willing to give the gift of forgiveness to receive it for ourselves.

When it comes to forgiveness, we can't hold others to a higher standard than we hold ourselves. Do we quickly expect forgiveness from others for everything we do; while at the same time are slow to offer forgiveness to others?

"But if ye forgive not men their trespasses, neither will your Father forgive your trespasses."
Matthew 6:15 KJV

The Bible teaches us to forgive others and ourselves as God has forgiven us. As long as our life doesn't get consumed with our mistakes; we can still forgive despite our mistakes. Forgiveness heals a hole that is in our souls and allows our hearts to be able to love unconditionally as Jesus does.

POSITIVE POWER PRAYER

Dear Lord, I thank you for this day. I thank you for this moment of knowing that I am being thought of in a positive and loving way by others who are reading this at this exact moment. Bless me with the Power of Forgiveness and the ability to forgive not only others but myself as well. Help me to understand that the Power of Forgiveness is in the asking to be forgiven and the ability to offer and give forgiveness to those who ask for it. And it is only by offering forgiveness that we are forgiven. Amen.

Eugenia Johnson-Smith

POSITIVE POWER STUDY

Who do you need to forgive?

_____
_____
_____
_____

Are you ready today to offer your forgiveness?
____Yes____No____Maybe

If Yes – When?(Date/Time)

_____

If No or Maybe - What is holding you back?

_____
_____
_____
_____

How will you feel once you have granted your forgiveness?

_____
_____
_____
_____

POSITIVE POWER

Who do you need to ask for forgiveness?
_____
_____
_____
_____
_____

How will you feel if they don't forgive you?
_____
_____
_____
_____
_____
_____
_____
_____
_____
_____
_____
_____
_____
_____
_____

Eugenia Johnson-Smith

Notes:

POSITIVE POWER

DEVOTION ELEVEN

The Power of I Can

"I can do all things through Christ who gives me strength,"
Philippians 4:13 NKJV

This is one of my favorite bible verses. If no one ever told you that you couldn't do something, you would have no reason to believe you couldn't do it. I can do all things and so can you! These are the words I live by and instill in my clients.

I have used this bible verse often when teaching at my church and in my day-to-day life. However, Thanksgiving 2015 offered a challenge to it. My niece shared that she was going to take part in the Kentucky Derby Half-Marathon the following April and suggested I join her. Well, neither of us was a runner and even if we were, neither of us had ever run 13.1 miles or even thought about it. I don't think I have ever run over five miles. Shoot, I don't even think I had ever run 1 mile without stopping. So I thought to myself, there is no way in the world I would say "yes" to that request. Did she really think I was crazy?

"I can do all things through Christ," came into my mind that very instant. And I thought, is that all it is? Just a favorite Bible verse? Or, do I really believe what the Word says? So, I took it as a sign and said "I *can* do this, and I *can* do all things through Christ who strengthens me." What a great witness this would be once completed! So I agreed to sign up to run the race with her. Oh did I forget to mention the race was about six months away?

Because we started our training in the winter, she and I trained first with walking CDs at home and at our YMCA--utilizing both the indoor walking track and treadmills. Once spring arrived and the weather improved, we started running outside. We continued to increase our run distance each week as race day grew closer. The next few weeks seemed to fly by.

It was time for the race and we were excited about our very first half-marathon. Our training had not gone as planned, or as well as we had hoped because our longest run was only six miles. But that was about halfway so no problem; we thought it would be okay!

Race weekend was finally here! It's customary to pick up race packets the day before the race and attend the Running Wild Expo, which is filled with all things running. It is also a place to learn about future races, purchase the latest in running gear, and document your accomplishment with photos and keepsakes.

Race morning, the excitement was so great, I asked myself, "Am I really doing this? I can't believe I'm actually running a half-marathon." I was not alone, there were 15,000 runners registered for this race, and they were from all over the United States. I was one of them, little ole me, a first-time half-marathon runner.

I started out the race with my niece and we were going at a steady pace, running together through neighborhoods, through parks, and around the track at Churchill Downs. As we ran around the race track, audio of past Kentucky Derby Races filled the air. We heard the call of Kentucky Derby winners; Secretariat, Affirmed, and Winning Colors over the public address system. I had never attended the Kentucky Derby, so I was in awe of the atmosphere of the grandstand, the twin spires, and seeing racehorses practicing as we ran around the infield of the track. It was like nothing I had ever experienced before.

After about six miles or so, I was on my own. My niece had run ahead and left me behind. At that very moment, I felt abandoned and isolated even in the midst of thousands of runners. I was upset because I thought, "How dare you leave me when it was your idea to run in this race in the first place?" I was having a "woe is me" moment, my very own private pity party. We were supposed to be running this race together. But there I was alone. It was at this moment that I needed her encouragement the most.

My legs felt like I was running in wet cement, and my lungs felt as if they were about to burst with each breath I took. Though my pace was slow I kept going. I didn't stop. I couldn't stop even as walkers passed me by. I could hear words of doubt and negativity trying to creep into my head; "You're not a runner. You'll never finish this race. Just give up and go home." I felt like I was moving backward in slow motion. But

POSITIVE POWER

I kept going, one foot in front of the other. I could barely hear it but it was there, the voice inside my head. "I got you." "You can do this." "I am with you." My legs started to feel lighter with each stride. Though my breath was still labored, my lungs no longer felt like they were going to explode.

Then after a few minutes, I pulled myself together and realized this half-marathon had never been about my niece at all. It had been about me. It was about my faith and my belief that I can do all things through Christ. I had to run my race. I had to finish my race. This would prove that I truly believed that I could do all things with Christ. Because that would be the only way I could run 13.1 miles.

So I picked up my bruised pride, picked up my pace, and started to run to the finish line with a new sense of purpose and determination. As I continued to run, I ran under a train trestle that had a banner on it that read, "I can do all things through Christ," and I thought, "Yes I Can" and "Yes I will." "Thank you, Jesus! "Wow! I got this!" After about 3 hours and 20 minutes, I crossed the finish line and received my very first half-marathon finisher's medal. That was such an awesome feeling. I felt exhausted, excited and powerful all at the same time. I did it! But I didn't run the race alone. It was the power of Christ within me that gave me what I needed to finish my race. I did It! Yes, with Christ I can do *all* things, and so can you. You have the power!

I signed up to run next year's Kentucky Derby Half-Marathon alone! My niece was unable to participate. It was important to me to run this time, to prove to myself that I could do it for me. The first time, it was her idea. I now love to run and have been running ever since. To date, I have run ten half-marathons.

I'm a runner! Who would have thought that? Not me. Now I am a part of a select group who get up early before the sun comes up to run. I am in the group of "those people," the ones you think are crazy for running in the rain. Neither I nor the "rainy day runners" are crazy. We just won't let a little rain stop us. So, if there is something you have always wanted to do, go with God and do it! You have the power to do it. You have the power of I can.

POSITIVE POWER PRAYER

Dear Lord, I thank you for this day. I thank you for this moment of knowing that I am being thought of in a positive and loving way by others who are reading this at this exact moment. I also thank you for the Power Of I Can! Help me to remember that I can do All things with you and that I remember that Me plus You Is Positive Power! Amen.

Eugenia Johnson-Smith

POSITIVE POWER STUDY

List three things you have always wanted to do.
1)_____
Goal date _____

2)_____
Goal date _____

3)_____
Goal date _____

I will not be stopped. I have the Power of I Can and I Will

_____
_____
_____
_____
_____
_____
_____
_____
_____
_____
_____
_____

POSITIVE POWER

Notes:

Eugenia Johnson-Smith

DEVOTIONAL TWELVE

The Power of If

"I sought the Lord, and he heard me and delivered me from all my fears."
Psalm 34:4 KJV

If not me then who?

Who will do it if I don't?

Who will do it if I won't?

Who will do it if I shan't?

Who will do it if I can't?

Who will do it without a dime?

Who will do it without any time?

"If" is one of the smallest words in the dictionary, yet we give it this great big influence and power over our lives. Why do we let it control us? What is it about this tiny little word that we fear? We need not fear the "If". He has the power to turn our "Ifs" around for good. With the power of "If" we could be unstoppable. If we work harder we could get a promotion or if we study harder we could earn that full academic scholarship we need.

It has no control over our lives. We are bigger than the wee little "If".

God didn't give us the spirit of fear. He gives us the courage to conquer little "Ifs" and great giants, no matter their form.

> *"Fear not, for I am with you; Be not dismayed, for I am your God. I will strengthen you, Yes, I will help you, I will uphold you with My righteous right hand."*
> *Isaiah 41:10 NKJV*

We have the power within us to overcome the "Ifs" in our lives. For example, --- If I had a degree I would be taken more seriously. If I had that promotion I could... If I got that raise I would be able to ....We can't let this little word paralyze us by stopping us from realizing, experiencing, and enjoying the full potential of our lives and of the life God wants us to have.

We have the power of a big God within us. He gives us courage to conquer our fears and to defeat our "Ifs".

Eugenia Johnson-Smith

POSITIVE POWER PRAYER

Dear Lord, I thank you for this day. I thank you for this moment of knowing that I am being thought of in a positive and loving way by others who are reading this at this exact moment. Thank you for granting me the ability to take the power over the "Ifs" in my life. They will no longer have power over me to stop me from living my dreams and reaching the full potential of my life. Amen.

POSITIVE POWER STUDY

What are the "Ifs" in your life?

Take a moment to think and to fill in the blanks:

If I were smarter I would:
_____
_____
_____
_____
_____

If I were richer I would:
_____
_____
_____
_____
_____

If I were bigger I would:
_____
_____
_____
_____
_____

If I were smaller I would:
_____
_____
_____
_____
_____

Eugenia Johnson-Smith

If I were braver I would:

_____
_____
_____
_____

If I had more time I would:

_____
_____
_____

If I had more friends I would:

_____
_____
_____
_____

If I said "no" more I could:

_____
_____
_____
_____
_____
_____
_____

POSITIVE POWER

If I rested more I could:

I will get smarter and I will:

I will get richer and I will:

I will get bigger and I will:

Eugenia Johnson-Smith

I will get smaller and I will:

_____
_____
_____
_____
_____

I will get braver and I will:

_____
_____
_____
_____
_____

I will make more time and I will:

_____
_____
_____
_____
_____
_____
_____

I will make more friends and I will:

_____
_____
_____
_____

POSITIVE POWER

I will say "no" more so I can:

___

I will rest more so I can:

___

Eugenia Johnson-Smith

I will:

I will:

I will:

POSITIVE POWER

Notes:

Eugenia Johnson-Smith

DEVOTION THIRTEEN

The Power of Impact

"Therefore be imitators of God, as beloved children."
Ephesians 5:1 ESV

We don't realize how much of an impact we have on others. Think about it. We go about our day-to-day lives in our own worlds, following our own agendas. Going from morning to night, sometimes on autopilot. When asked, "What did you do all day?" We often can't remember. We don't remember who we saw, who we spoke to, or who we passed by without a glance or a word. But our presence impacts each person we come into contact with and it is felt by them whether we realize it or not.

Nowadays we are so busy checking email, Facebook, Instagram, and other social media that we don't even have time for face-to-face or voice-to-voice communication. Other times, we are so busy looking at our smartphones that we ignore those that mean the most to us.

POSITIVE POWER

Can you put the phone down and get off social media for a while? What do you fear you will miss? There was life before smartphones. There was life before you had to inform every one of your Facebook friends where you are at this very moment and share photos of your location or half-eaten meal.

Whether on social media or in person, every interaction is a seed of impact in the lives of those we encounter - seeds that, if positive, can grow into beautiful flowers of hope and possibility. But if they are negative, they can grow into giant weeds of pain and destruction. Weeds can sometimes get out of control and lead to destructive behaviors.

Are you conscious of how you interact with family, friends, classmates, co-workers, or even strangers? The thing is people notice you whether you see them or not. Your actions matter, whether they are positive or negative. They impact the lives of everyone you come into contact with, those on social media and those in person.

When you post on social media you are planting seeds that continue to grow and spread with every share.

We have no idea of what's going on in our heads or in the lives of those we come in contact with every day, or even those we live with.
Are you sowing seeds of encouragement or seeds of destruction into their lives?

"Be not deceived: evil communication corrupt good manners."
1 Corinthians 15:33 KJV

Your actions and your words can be "the straw that breaks the camel's back" or they can be the inspiration that saves a lost soul.

There are people in our lives that are in pain and we don't even know it. How we treat people can hurt or help. The things we do and say can make a difference in the lives of those we come into contact with. These weeds or seeds of destruction may not manifest themselves immediately. They may take years but they can choke out what little bit of positive energy is left in their lives.

POSITIVE POWER

That's why we must treat every life we come in contact with as precious and as beloved. How do we do that, you ask? By sowing seeds of love, kindness, hopefulness, encouragement, and Positive Power. We may be the only light of hope they encounter in a day, week, month, or year. When we sow seeds of positive impact into their lives we create the ability to overcome weeds of negativity and destruction.

Eugenia Johnson-Smith

POSITIVE POWER PRAYER

Dear Lord, I thank you for this day. I thank you for this moment of knowing that I am being thought of in a positive and loving way by others who are reading this at this exact moment. Help me Lord to plant positive seeds of impact into all the lives I am blessed to touch. Amen.

POSITIVE POWER STUDY

What kind of impact do you have on others?

What kind of impact are you making on social media?

How are you planting seeds of positive impact in the lives of others?

Eugenia Johnson-Smith

What are some of the seeds you are planting?

What legacy are you leaving for the future?

POSITIVE POWER

Notes:

Eugenia Johnson-Smith

DEVOTIONAL FOURTEEN

The Power Of Letting Go

"A Time to get, and a time to lose; a time to keep, and a time to cast away;"
Ecclesiastes 3:6 KJV

TVs, computers, scanners, VCRs, and old electronics, are all not being used and taking up space. All obsolete and sitting around occupying prime real estate in my house. Well, really junking up and cluttering up my house. I walk past them almost every day. The spare bedroom that has become the collection room of all things unwanted, unused, or unneeded. The "storage room." "Wink wink." But let's just call it what it is.....The Junk Room!

Storage room sounds sooooooooo much better. I have asked myself, "What is all this stuff? Where did it come from? Why am I still holding on to it? Why am I letting it take up valuable space?" Usable space.

We all have them; junk rooms, junk closets, or junk drawers. Places we put stuff or junk we want to hide from our friends, our family, and

POSITIVE POWER

even ourselves. We hold on to physical junk or "STUFF", as my pastor says.

We also hold on to emotional junk that gunks up our spirits. This gunk clouds our spirit and dims our inner light, stopping it from shining at its full potential.

We may have unresolved anger issues from heartaches, from heartbreaks, abandonment pains, and the pains of losing a loved one.

You may be thinking that's not my problem. Maybe it's not. But you know there are some things in your life you need to release. You may be holding on to people or a job that is sucking the life out of you. They may be good people and the job may be a good job. But not good for you.

> "..., Thus saith the Lord,
> set thine house in order;..."
> 2 Kings 20:1 KJV

There comes a time in our lives when we just need to open our eyes, wide open, and take a good look at our current situation. Take an inventory of our "Stuff." Our physical "Stuff" and our emotional "Stuff" and let it go. When we let it go, our physical house and our spiritual house will be in order.

Some of the "Stuff" we are dealing with we may be able to let go of on our own. But there may be other "Stuff" we may need pastoral or professional assistance to let it go. Don't be afraid to get the help you need to let go of your physical or emotional "Stuff." You do not have to do it alone.

POSITIVE POWER

POSITIVE POWER PRAYER

Dear Lord, I thank you for this day. I thank you for this moment of knowing that I am being thought of in a positive and loving way by others who are reading this at this exact moment. I ask that you give me the strength and the positive power to let go of the things that have been holding me back from the life you have for me. I know it won't be easy, but I am willing and I am ready. Amen.

Eugenia Johnson-Smith

POSITIVE POWER STUDY

I'm ready to let go of my physical "Stuff."

I will let go of:

_____
_____
_____
_____
_____
_____
_____
_____
_____

Date:_____ I will let it go.

List people or organizations you can bless with the "Stuff" you no longer use, need or want.

_____
_____
_____
_____
_____
_____
_____
_____

POSITIVE POWER

How do you feel now that you have gotten rid of your "Stuff"?

_____
_____
_____
_____
_____

I'm ready to let go of my emotional "Stuff."

I will let go of:

_____
_____
_____
_____
_____
_____
_____
_____
_____
_____
_____
_____
_____
_____
_____
_____

How has holding on to this "Stuff" impacted your happiness?

_____
_____
_____
_____

How has holding on to this "Stuff" impacted your spiritual growth?

_____
_____
_____
_____

How will your life be better now without it?

_____
_____
_____
_____
_____
_____
_____
_____

POSITIVE POWER

If I need help I will ask:
_____

(It should be someone you trust, you can count on to hold you accountable as you work through this process.)

Eugenia Johnson-Smith

Notes:

DEVOTION FIFTEEN

The Power Of Listening

*"If one gives an answer before
he hears, it is his folly and shame."
Proverbs 18:13 KJV*

*"Be silent in the Lord's presence and
wait patiently for him. Don't be angry
because of the one whose way prospers
or the one who implements evil schemes."
Psalm 37:7 ISV*

You don't always have to speak. Find a quiet place. Sometimes you need to be still, to be quiet, and to just listen. Block out the noise, get away from people and turn off the electronic devices or even lock them away.

"Shhh! Can You Hear It?"

If you listen quietly, you can hear it.
Shhh, quiet please. It's the voice of God.

Shhh! Can You Hear It?

It's the voice that says, "Everything is going to be alright."

It's the voice that says, "You can do it. You can do all things with me."

Shhh! Can You Hear It?
It's the voice that says, "This too shall pass."
It's the voice that says, "You're not alone for I am with you always."

Shhh! Can You Hear It?
It's the voice that says, "Don't be afraid."
It's the voice that says, "Fear not, I have not given you the spirit of fear."

Shhh! Can You Hear It?
It's the voice of God.

When we share our problems with others our ears are open to their opinions. Many different voices saying different things. We can't understand what we hear. The sound is loud.

There's no way we can hear God through the noise. We must get quiet. When we listen and focus on what He is saying we will hear the

POSITIVE POWER

answer. We will know in our hearts that everything is going to be okay and that this situation will pass. No longer will we be afraid.

We heard Him say, "You can do it. You can do all things with me." His voice was loud and clear because we were silent.

Eugenia Johnson-Smith

POSITIVE POWER PRAYER

Dear Lord, I thank you for this day. I thank you for this moment of knowing that I am being thought of in a positive and loving way by others who are reading this at this exact moment. Let me calm my spirit so that I may hear your voice. Amen.

POSITIVE POWER STUDY

What questions do you need God to answer?
_____
_____
_____
_____
_____

How long have you been waiting?
_____
_____
_____
_____
_____

Where is your quiet space?
_____
_____
_____
_____
_____
_____
_____
_____

Eugenia Johnson-Smith

Are you ready to receive God's answer?

POSITIVE POWER

Notes:

Eugenia Johnson-Smith

DEVOTION SIXTEEN

The Power of Love

The Bible speaks of four types of love.
They are the Greek words
Eros, Storge, Philia and Agape.

"Love suffers long and is kind; love does not envy; love does not parade itself, is not puffed up; does not behave rudely, does not seek its own, is not provoked, thinks no evil; does not rejoice in iniquity, but rejoices truth; bears all thing, believes all things, hopes all things, endures all things. Love never fails...."
1 Corinthians 13:4-8 NKJV

What does it mean to love? What does it mean to be loved? What does it mean to be in love? What does it mean to give love? What does it mean to allow yourself to be loved? What does it mean to say love grows? What does it mean to have the Love of Christ? You may have heard the phrase love hurts. Should it? Does it?

Agape - God's Love,

It's Unconditional

POSITIVE POWER

"God so Loved the World that he gave his only begotten son that whosoever believed in Him should not perish but have everlasting life."
John 3:16   KJV

That's what it means to love.

I would say that when Jesus went to the cross for our sins, it hurt. He was nailed to the cross for our sins. He was also pierced in the side for our sins. He was whipped with leather straps embedded with glass and metal shards for our sins.

Just thinking about the pain he endured for me hurts. He never complained about it or asked for it to stop. I would say in this case, yes. Love hurts. That's what it means to *be loved.*

Philia - Platonic Love,

It's Friendship Love

There is no greater love than to give your life for a friend. Jesus freely gave His life for us. Could you give your life for a friend or someone you don't know? Could you give your life for someone who may not even care for you? That's what it means to g*ive love.*

Eugenia Johnson-Smith

"Greater love hath no man than this, that a man lay down his life for his friends."
John 15:13 KJV

Eros - Romantic Love,

It's The Love Between Couples

In the age of social media, I find myself texting and receiving texts from my husband all the time. I texted my husband while exercising, "What are you doing?" He texted back, "Falling in Love with you. "I texted him back, "you are making me smile really Big :) I Love You!" He texted back, "Love U :). "

Saying things out of the blue, that are unexpected, sweet, and nice. That's what it means to be *In Love.*

The emotions we were feeling during that text exchange are those that you can't put a price on. It's more precious than a $4 million diamond ring. True Love is more valuable than any material thing you could possess. Many with unlimited financial wealth have empty love banks.

POSITIVE POWER

The people you love, those that really love you will stop what they're doing and run to you in your time of need. You will gladly, freely no question give them your last of anything. That's what it means to g*ive love*. It doesn't hurt to say, "I Love You" from time to time either. That's my Love Story. What's yours?

Storge - Family Love,

It's A Parents' Love For Their Child

Parents start to love their children even before they are born. It is out of love that the idea of children is born. With the passing of time as parent and child bond over shared experiences, their l*ove grows*.

A parent's love is unconditional. A loving parent loves you no matter what the situation or circumstance you find yourself in. They love you if you are good, bad, right, or wrong. They love you when you love them and when you don't love them. They love you in spite of you and they love you because of you. You are their child. That's unconditional love. That's the Love of Christ. He Loves us in spite of our sinful nature, and in spite of how we treat him. He

Eugenia Johnson-Smith

Loves us when we forget to thank Him for all He has done and continues to do for us. He loves us even when we don't have time for Him. Christ's Love is non-judgmental.

Are you caring for a sick relative? Are you hanging in with a loved one who has had an addiction of some kind that seems like a lifetime? Are you honoring your vow of love through sickness and health? Are you supporting a loved one who is in prison whether it is behind bars or in the prison of their mind? Are you supporting a loved one who has lost a job, savings, home, dignity, or hope? Because you vowed to love for richer and for poorer. When we love, when we truly love, we love unconditionally. We love people, not the things they have or for what they can give us. True unconditional love has no strings attached. I love you because of who you are even when you don't love me.

Let us take time to say these three little words, "I Love You." Three words that have a big meaning to those in our lives we love: our parents, children, husbands, wives, significant others, siblings, etc. You may be thinking they know I Love them so why do I have to say it?

POSITIVE POWER

Because we need to hear it! And if you are good at saying it, you also need to be good at showing it. If you are new to expressing Love it will be important that your words and your actions line up. You want to make sure you are being consistent with your message. You must show and verbalize your Love!

Eugenia Johnson-Smith

POSITIVE POWER PRAYER

Dear Lord, I thank you for this day, I thank you for this moment of knowing that I am being thought of in a positive and loving way by others who are reading this at this exact moment. I also thank you for the Power To Love! Grant me the Power of Unselfish, Unconditional, Unstoppable, Unwavering, and Unyielding Love. Let me have the Love of Christ in my heart and let me live each day by his example of showing Love and Charity. Amen.

POSITIVE POWER STUDY

What does it mean to you To Love?

___

What does it mean to you to Be Loved?

___

What does it mean to you to be In Love?

___

Eugenia Johnson-Smith

What does it mean to you to Give Love?

What does it mean to you to say Love Grows?

What does it mean to you to have the Love of Christ?

POSITIVE POWER

Notes:

Eugenia Johnson-Smith

DEVOTION SEVENTEEN

The Power Of Peace

War and peace, wars and rumors of war are phrases we have heard many times. Wars that used to be fought in distant far away lands are now fought right here on our very own doorsteps.

It seems that if we look at the images received via television, they have us believing there is no hope of peace. We are at war with other countries. We are at war with those of the opposite sex. We are at war with those of different political parties. We are at war with other religions. We are even at war within our own families. We are fighting so many battles, it seems we are at war with everyone. Can we ever have peace?

Where is the peace that surpasses all understanding? Where did the peace go? Will there ever be peace? Do we truly want peace? Or, are we systematically doing things that prevent true peace from ever becoming a reality? These seem like million dollar questions. But can we put a price on peace?

POSITIVE POWER

*"If you're not part of the Solution,
You're part of the problem."
African Proverb*

Which are you?

We are supposed to be a peaceful nation built on the principles of "In God we Trust" and "... one Nation under God indivisible, with liberty and justice for all." This is expressed in our Pledge of Allegiance to the Flag and on our national currency. Yet we can't get along with our fellow man, or our brothers and sisters from another mother.

*"...Thou shalt love thy
neighbor as thyself."
Matthew 22:39 KJV*

"Peace I leave with you, my peace I give unto you; not as the world giveth, give I unto you.

*Let not your heart be troubled,
neither let it be afraid."
John 14:27 KJV*

The lack of unity and love has caused the loss of our peace of mind. Our safe havens no longer exist. Parents worry when they send their children off to school every day, for fear they may not return at day's end. Gone are the days of mindless shopping trips to the mall, or being carefree at a concert or sporting event. Our sense of security relies on metal detectors or hand-held wands when entering schools, concerts or sporting events.

"United we stand, divided we fall" -- Motto of the Commonwealth of Kentucky

For years churches have been known as places of shelter or sanctuary, when there was no other place of safe refuge. But now, even our houses of worship are not immune to society's misguided thoughts and rhetoric. Our place of peace has been corrupted. Our peaceful spirit is now shaken, and our sense of security has been taken away. It has been replaced by thoughts of those who lost their lives in their places of worship.

We have become a society on heightened alert at all times. We are suspicious of a lone bag at an airport and have insecure thoughts when we see someone who we think fits a preconceived terrorist profile.

There is still hope for peace!

All hearts are not hardened.

Hearts can be changed.

POSITIVE POWER

Peace can be achieved.

When we peel off our outer shell, of clothing, of skin color, of gender, of religion, of political affiliation, we are all the same... blood, sweat, and tears. We bleed when we are cut. We sweat when we work hard. We cry when we are hurt or lose a loved one. We all breathe the same air.

When we all sit at the same table, acknowledge our differences and seek to understand the different cultures and opinions we may be surprised that we have things in common and can work towards peace. We all want to feel safe. We want our children to grow up and to have a better life than ours. Our children's future could be the key to peace.

When we start to focus on our commonalities, our differences fade away into a distant memory. We will be able to celebrate our diversities and honor what each has to offer. Love and Kindness will fill our hearts and unity will be produced. Where there is unity, there is the Power of Peace.

*"Endeavoring to keep the unity of the
Spirit in the bond of peace."
Ephesians 4:3 KJV*

There's a perfect peace in the Lord. It's the kind of peace you can only get from him. The kind that can calm a storm or raging sea with the wave of a hand or a few words. It's the power of His peace that surpasses all understanding. He is the Prince of Peace and He is the key to our peace. The answer is yes.

We will find the Power of Peace!

POSITIVE POWER PRAYER

Dear Lord, I thank you for this day. I thank you for this moment of knowing that I am being thought of in a positive and loving way by others who are reading this at this exact moment. Lord, I know that you need only say the word and there will be peace. You have the power to calm the angry sea with your words. I pray for your Power Of Peace to touch the hearts and minds of all mankind. Amen.

Eugenia Johnson-Smith

POSITIVE POWER STUDY

What does peace look like to you today?

_____
_____
_____
_____
_____
_____

When or where do you feel most vulnerable?

_____
_____
_____
_____
_____
_____

When do you believe peace will be achieved?

_____
_____
_____
_____
_____
_____
_____
_____

POSITIVE POWER

How are you contributing to the solution of peace?

___

What does the Bible verse, Matthew 22:39 mean to you?

___

Eugenia Johnson-Smith

Where do you need peace?

POSITIVE POWER

Notes:

Eugenia Johnson-Smith

DEVOTION EIGHTEEN

The Power Of Renewal

"Therefore if any man be in Christ, he is a new creature; old things are passed away; behold, new things are become new."
2 Corinthians 5:17 KJV

The New Year is a time people focus on renewal. The anticipation of the New Year brings thoughts of past resolutions that never got resolved. It ushers in a new year, with new possibilities and a time to focus on new resolutions. Most of which we don't even keep through the end of the day. Some do better and can make it to the end of the month. Still, others make it through summer while others can't even tell you what they had resolved to do.

The New Year is not the only time for renewal. We don't need to wait until January 1st to experience our renewal. Every day can be a day of renewal. Each sunrise is the dawn of a new beginning and the opportunity for renewal.

POSITIVE POWER

We can make a new start or new commitment any time we choose. Think about it. How many times have you started or restarted a "diet", quit smoking, or said you were leaving an abusive relationship? It doesn't matter how many times you did in the past. The past is the past. We are talking about today. What are the things you choose to recommit to doing from this day forward?

Do you need to renew a relationship with your parents, children, spouse, or significant other? Is it time to mend the fences of broken relationships? Do you need to offer an olive branch or wave the white flag of surrender for a war that has gone on way too long, so long that no one remembers how it started? Do the words "I'm sorry" or "I forgive you" need to be spoken?

Before you start this journey of renewal, take some time to reflect on the reasons you were unable to follow through in the past. There may be unresolved emotional issues that are blocking your ability to succeed or issues you may not have considered.

Take some time to reflect on the reason it is important for you to make these positive changes in your life. The only way you will succeed is if you are doing this for the right reason. Only you know the right reason. It's not your family's reason, your friend's reason, or society's reason. It's not anyone else's reason, but yours. When it is your reason, no one can stand in the way of your success.

Here's a thought, to paraphrase words I remember from my desk calendar…"Within you lies a place of happiness and a place of renewal. To reach it you must withdraw your attention from the world outside and focus on the strength and energy inside of you."

No matter how much we try, we can't control other people. Sometimes we spend so much energy and time trying to do this that we miss our blessings and peace. We can only control how we react to outside forces in our lives. It is only through personal growth and renewal that we are able to understand this.

POSITIVE POWER PRAYER

Dear Lord, I thank you for this day. I thank you for this moment of knowing that I am being thought of in a positive and loving way by others who are reading this at this exact moment. Help me to find within myself the Power of Renewal so that I can start to rebuild and renew relationships and begin to recommit to living my best life. Amen.

POSITIVE POWER STUDY

What does your own life of renewal look like?

_____
_____
_____
_____
_____

What do you really think about the life you have led thus far?

_____
_____
_____
_____
_____
_____

What relationship do you need to repair?

_____
_____
_____
_____
_____
_____
_____
_____

POSITIVE POWER

What are your resolutions?

Eugenia Johnson-Smith

Notes:

To serve patients

POSITIVE POWER

DEVOTION NINETEEN

The Power Of Your Purpose

*"Each of you should use whatever
gift you have received to serve others,
as faithful stewards of God's
grace in its various forms."*
1 Peter 4:10 NIV

We are all the same yet different in our own way. We are all born into this world, breathe, bleed and eventually die. Some will have long lives and others not so long. Some lives will be eventful, some not so eventful. Long, short, eventful, uneventful. What measure do we use? What's the standard?

How do you measure a life? Does the number of years lived determine a good life? If you live to the ripe old age of 80, 90, or 100, is that the measure of a good life? What if you are only blessed with 10, 20, or 30 years of life? Is that the measure of a good life? When we speak of a good life it can't just be determined by the years we live.

We must take into account the quality of life. What have we done with our lives? What are we doing with our lives? What are we planning to do with our lives in the future? The answers to these questions will determine if the life we have lived is a good life.

We, like animals, were all created by God with a purpose. Some animals were created to feed us, help us work the land, and provide transportation, while others help to clean the environment. In the book "The Purpose Driven Life" by Pastor Rick Warren, he states, "We all have a purpose in life, and that we are to have the inner peace that God intended."

"And we know that all things work together for good to them that love God, to them who are the called according to his purpose." Romans 8:28 KJV

What is your purpose or calling? How do you know what it is? You may not be able to identify it at this moment but recognize that you do have a calling on your life. You are meant to be of service to someone. It may be on a world scale, or it may be only in your local community.

POSITIVE POWER

Do a self-assessment of the things that give you joy, the things you would do for free, and the things you are passionate about. Take an inventory of your skills and talents. You may already be doing them.

Do you love to cook? Do you get joy out of seeing people enjoying your food creations? Your calling could be to feed the homeless by working in or running a "Soup Kitchen."

Do you enjoy carpentry? Do you like to build things? Habitat for Humanity could be a place to serve. You don't even have to be a professional carpenter to help. You need only the passion and desire to help. There are also organizations that build ramps for wheelchair access to private homes for veterans.

Are you a good listener, non-judgmental, and can keep confidence? You could be the caring voice on the phone of a "Help Line."

Still not sure? Take some time and really think about it. Pray, meditate on it, sit quietly and listen. You will eventually hear your calling. Just be ready to answer it.

Eugenia Johnson-Smith

POSITIVE POWER PRAYER

Dear Lord, I thank you for this day. I thank you for this moment of knowing that I am being thought of in a positive and loving way by others who are reading this at this exact moment. Lord, I open my heart, my mind, and my spirit to receive the calling you have placed upon my life. I acknowledge the Power Of Purpose and I'm ready, willing, and able to serve. Amen.

POSITIVE POWER STUDY

List three things that bring you joy.

1)_____
_____
_____

2)_____
_____
_____

3)_____
_____
_____

How can the above three things be used to serve others?

_____
_____
_____
_____
_____
_____
_____

Select one or two of the three to put into action.

What positive impact will this have on the lives of others?

POSITIVE POWER

Notes:

Eugenia Johnson-Smith

DEVOTION TWENTY

The Power of Thank You

"In every thing give thanks; for this is the will of God in Christ Jesus concerning you."
1 Thessalonians 5:18 KJV

Thank you. Two little words that have a big meaning and are important to speak and hear. Are these words part of your everyday vocabulary? If they aren't, they should be.

How many times do you wish your boss had said, "Thank you" for a job well done? We work hard and we work long hours to meet the deadlines others have placed on us. We make sacrifices for the benefit of others, yet our sacrifices are not even noticed.

Do any of these statements resonate with you? I'm the one who makes the coffee and gets the pastries every day. I'm the one who gets the kids up, fed, and to school on time. I'm the one who is the taxi for the neighborhood kids to and from practices and activities. I don't mind it, but every now and then a simple "Thank You" would be so nice to hear. It helps give us that power we need to continue to do those things.

At times do you feel you are being taken advantage of or even taken for granted? Do those around you just assume you will do whatever is asked, without even asking about your availability? Appreciation goes a long way and is simple to show. It can be verbalized, it can be a simple Thank You card or it can be a personalized hand-written Thank You note. Personally, I love the latter. It's special and it shows the time and effort of the sender. Don't get hung up on the type. The important thing is that you are receiving a thank you. Whether it be via email, text message, or voice mail, the sentiment is still the same.

When we receive our thank you no matter the form we should accept it with grace and gratitude. We should appreciated the time they took to offer the thank you.

> *"O give thanks unto the Lord; for he is good;*
> *for his mercy endureth for ever."*
> *1 Chronicles 16:34 KJV*

We have been concentrating on you as the receiver of the Thank You. How are you at thanking others? When was the last time you said Thank You to someone? Was it today, yesterday or so long ago you can't remember? It's never too late to express thanks. Here are a few examples ---- Drop a note in your mailbox for your mailman. It will let him know how much you appreciate him for delivering your mail in the rain and snow. You could send pizzas, after a large snowfall, to the city workers who are responsible for snow removal. They are out all hours of the day and night removing the snow, so the roads are safe for your travel. How about coffee and doughnuts for the office of sanitation? They are up way before the sun comes up, collecting our garbage and keeping the city clean. These are but a few gestures that could make their day. I'm sure you can think of many more people who deserve your thanks.

It's good to show gratitude and appreciation. It's extra special when it is given to those who often feel unseen. Expressions of thanks are validation that they are valued.

Do you thank God for all he has done for you? Is He on the list of those you are taking for granted? Do you thank Him for the power to get out of bed, for a sound mind, and for the people who love you? It doesn't matter the size of the blessing, big or small they all deserve to be acknowledged with a Thank You. We sometimes are so busy living our lives that we forget to give thanks to the one who holds our lives in His hands.

He does so much that we often take our blessings for granted and don't acknowledge his protection, his love, his grace and mercy and his gift of salvation. He deserves our sincere thanks every second of every day. It should be the first thing we say in the morning and the last think we say at night. Thank you Lord for all you do and have done for me.

When we live our lives in service and in a way that pleases God we are showing him thanks. When we acknowledge our blessings or bear witness to the things God has done for us we are giving him thanks.

Eugenia Johnson-Smith

POSITIVE POWER PRAYER

Dear Lord, I thank you for this day. I thank you for this moment of knowing that I am being thought of in a positive and loving way by others who are reading this at this exact moment. Please help me to take the time to say Thank You to those I may have overlooked. Help me to be aware of the need for others to hear the words Thank You and of the power of letting people know they are appreciated. Amen.

POSITIVE POWER STUDY

Who in your day-to-day life are you taking for granted?

_____
_____
_____
_____
_____

List the people you will thank.

_____
_____
_____
_____
_____
_____
_____
_____
_____
_____
_____
_____
_____
_____

Eugenia Johnson-Smith

How will you make saying Thank You an important part of your life?

_____
_____
_____
_____
_____

Why is it important to say Thank You to your family, friends and general public?

_____
_____
_____
_____
_____
_____
_____
_____
_____
_____
_____
_____
_____
_____
_____
_____

POSITIVE POWER

Notes:

Eugenia Johnson-Smith

DEVOTION TWENTY-ONE

The Power Of Words

"Sticks and Stones can break my bones but words can never hurt me." I learned that little quote early in life. But it is not entirely true. I know the intent of the quote was to discourage physical confrontations by encouraging diplomacy and instilling compromise. But words can sometimes hurt you.

There is Power in words. We have the power to speak things into our destiny or manifest them into truth.

"For as he thinketh in his heart, so is he:...,"
Proverbs 23:7 KJV

Hearing something over and over again, day in and day out, it starts to take hold of your thoughts and become ingrained in your mind and spirit, thus becoming your truth. Hearing and being exposed to negative or positive words can lead to a negative or positive mindset or outlook on life.

POSITIVE POWER

Research indicates that women speak about 20,000 words a day on average while men speak only 7,000. That's about 860.3 million words in a lifetime. That's a whole lot of words. We can reason that out of all those millions some of them could be bad words, hurtful words, or negative words. Words that could most likely go unspoken. While on the other hand, some of those millions of words could be good words, encouraging words, and positive power words. Words that should be spoken, spoken often, and spoken out loud.

How many times have you felt you've said too much, didn't say enough, could have said more, or should have kept your mouth shut altogether? Words big, little, long, short - they have power. Power to create and power to destroy! In the beginning, God said, Let there be light and there was Light! Power! Words once spoken can not be recalled. Like a pebble dropped into a pond, it has a ripple effect and it goes on and on and on.

We are created by God and his Positive Power dwells within us. He gives us guidance in his word, on how we are to use the very special and powerful gift we have: the ability to speak.

Eugenia Johnson-Smith

"The tongue has the power of life and death, and those who love it will eat its fruit."
Proverbs 18:21 NIV

We must be mindful of the words we speak. Are they kind, supportive, encouraging, comforting, or helpful?

We must be mindful of how we speak. The tone used. How does it fall on the delicate or sensitive ears of others? Was it received in the same spirit it was spoken?

We must be mindful of when to speak. Before we speak, ask the question. Should I speak or should I be silent and hold my tongue?

Use your words for good, not evil. Use words to uplift, inspire and encourage others and to help them along the way.

We mustn't misuse or take our ability to speak for granted. Some do not have that ability.

POSITIVE POWER PRAYER

Dear Lord, I thank you for this day. I thank you for this moment of knowing that I am being thought of in a positive and loving way by others who are reading this at this exact moment. I acknowledge that my words have power and I will be responsible with the words I choose to speak in my life and into the lives of others. I ask that you will help guide me in choosing the right words for the situation. Amen.

Eugenia Johnson-Smith

POSITIVE POWER STUDY

What words have hurt you?

_____
_____
_____
_____
_____

How do the words make you feel?

_____
_____
_____
_____
_____

What words have you used that have hurt others?

_____
_____
_____
_____
_____

How do you think it made them feel?

_____
_____

POSITIVE POWER

Why is it important for you to choose your words wisely?

_____
_____
_____
_____
_____
_____

How can you encourage others to make better word choices?

_____
_____
_____
_____
_____
_____
_____
_____
_____

How will you share the importance of understanding the Power of Words?

_____
_____
_____

Eugenia Johnson-Smith

Notes:

POSITIVE POWER

DEVOTION TWENTY-TWO

The Power of Your Inner Voice

Jesus looked at them and said, *"With man this is impossible, but with God all things are possible."*
Matthew 19:26 NIV

Who Said? And Who Are The "Theys"?

Who said, You couldn't do that?
Who said, You shouldn't go there?
Who said, You can't do that?
Who said, You won't amount to anything?
Who said, You're too small or too tall to do that?

They said, "I'm not good enough."
They said, "I'm not smart enough."
They said, "I'm not good-looking enough."
They said, "I'm not talented enough."

I am good enough because God made me and he made everything Good!

God's word encourages us and speaks to us saying, "but with God All things are possible."

Not some things. All Things! His word gives us Power. The Power to quiet the *theys* in our lives. Who are *They* and why are we listening to them anyway? You are the captain on this voyage and this is the journey of your life so...

What do You say you can do?
Where do You say you can go?
What do You say you are good enough for?
What do You say you are smart enough for?
What do You say you are talented enough to do?
What do You say you will accomplish?

Listen To Your Inner Voice.
Silence the "Theys."
You have the Power: You Decide!

Listen to your voice, the voice that has hope, the voice that sees the awesome opportunities life has to offer. Listen to the voice that says, "I will not be defeated. God has my back. I can do anything I set my mind to do. I have dreams. I will set goals. I will accomplish them with determination and hard work."

POSITIVE POWER PRAYER

Dear Lord, I thank you for this day. I thank you for this moment of knowing that I am being thought of in a positive and loving way by others who are reading this at this exact moment. I also thank you for the ability of the Power Of My Inner Voice to drown out the "Theys" in my life. Help me to remember that there is nothing too big for You and that I have Your Power living within me. Teach me to be quiet and listen for your voice and allow it to guide my life. Amen.

Eugenia Johnson-Smith

POSITIVE POWER STUDY

What is your voice saying to you?

_____
_____
_____
_____
_____

What will you do?

_____
_____
_____
_____
_____

What are your talents?

_____
_____
_____
_____
_____

How are you using your talents?

_____
_____
_____
_____

POSITIVE POWER

What are your goals?

_____
_____
_____
_____
_____
_____
_____
_____
_____
_____
_____

What things in your life seemed impossible; now with God are possible?

_____
_____
_____
_____
_____
_____
_____
_____
_____
_____

DEVOTION TWENTY-THREE

Power Of The Eagle

"But they that wait upon the Lord shall renew their strength; they shall mount up with wings as eagles; they shall run, and not be weary; and they shall walk, and not faint."
Isaiah 30:31 KJV

E Elevate yourself above discouragement, negativity, or anything that is blocking your way. Eagles have the ability to soar high above mountains.

What are the mountains in your life? Know that once you are above them you can see past them and they will no longer block your view or your way. That means they can no longer stand in your way or stop you from achieving your goals in life.

A Achieve Once you understand that you can elevate yourself over any and all obstacles that are placed in your path, you will be able to achieve your dreams and start to SOAR towards your life goals - the desires of your heart.

POSITIVE POWER

*"Therefore I tell you, whatever
you ask for in prayer, believe that
you have received it, and it will be yours."*
Mark 11:24 NIV

G Goals In order to SOAR like an ***Eagle***, you must set goals. These goals should be measurable; you must be able to know when the goal is achieved. Make sure to have both short-term and long-term goals. This will allow you to have a successful journey to your ultimate goal without becoming discouraged by doubt and negativity. It is okay to ask for help from others, family, friends, co-workers, spiritual guides, and anyone who is considered a supporter or a cheerleader.

L Lead You must be like the ***Eagle*** that SOARs above mediocrity and the ordinary seeking to reach the highest of heights. They are not your ordinary birds. They make their nests on the high mountains, never losing sight of those below. Like the ***Eagle*** you must keep your eye on your followers, making sure they are still following no matter if they are following closely or far. In order to lead you must have those who believe in you and are willing to follow you. As such, a good leader encourages and mentors his followers preparing them to one day take his place.

E Educate it is important to get as much education as you can in order to reach your goals and to never stop learning. A good leader is one who shares his or her knowledge. The more you know the more you can help yourself and others. It is important to share what you learn. When you help others everyone succeeds.

The Power of The ***Eagle*** was inspired by and dedicated to my niece Shaleigha in whom I see great strength, power, courage, passion, boldness, determination, motivation, and compassion. I would tell her as a kindergartner, "Don't stay on the ground with the chickens, soar like the Eagle you are." From then on I called her "Little Eagle." She has grown into a beautiful young lady both inside and out. She graduated college, received her masters with honors and has held many leadership roles. She will always be my "Little Eagle." Who are the Little Eagles in your life? Identify them and start to sow the seeds of promise, the seeds of encouragement, and the seeds of inspiration into their lives. Embrace The Power of the Eagle!

POSITIVE POWER PRAYER

Dear Lord, I thank you for this day. I thank you for this moment of knowing that I am being thought of in a positive and loving way by others who are reading this at this exact moment. I also thank you for the Power of the Eagle! Help me to remember that I have the Power to Elevate myself above any situation that comes my way. I know I can Achieve the desires of my heart because it says so in your word. I will wait on you Lord knowing that I will reach My Goals. I know as a Leader those I lead may not always want to follow but I <u>Will Not</u> get weary for I will continue to lead by your example Lord and Educate them in your ways. Amen.

Eugenia Johnson-Smith

POSITIVE POWER STUDY

Who are the "Little Eagles" in your life?

_____
_____
_____
_____
_____
_____

What are you doing to cultivate them?

_____
_____
_____
_____
_____
_____
_____
_____

How are you inspiring them?

_____
_____
_____
_____
_____
_____

POSITIVE POWER

How are you leading them?

_____
_____
_____
_____

How are you encouraging them to Soar?

_____
_____
_____
_____
_____
_____
_____
_____
_____
_____
_____

What are you teaching them?

_____
_____
_____
_____

Eugenia Johnson-Smith

Notes:

POSITIVE POWER

DEVOTION TWENTY-FOUR

The Power of the Light

"You are the light of the world. A city that is set on a hill cannot be hid."
Matthew 5:14 KJV

I believe we all have a light inside of us; we're all born with it. Some of us know we have it. Some of us are told we have it by those who see it within us. Those who see it could be family, friends, teachers, co-workers, or even mentors who encourage the growth of our light.

How do you know you have it, you ask? By your talk, your walk, and your actions or your lack of actions. As Christians, you are to let your light shine so those around you see the good you do and how it honors God. This means you help those in need as Jesus did without judgment. It doesn't matter if you feel you are a good person or not, you were born with the light. You just need to be willing to activate it.

Those who don't realize they have it can be compared to someone in a dark room with a flashlight. No one ever told them what the flashlight could do, what it was for, or even how to use it. They are in the dark and will stay in the dark until they learn how the flashlight works and can turn it on.

Others enter the room or enter your life with the same light you have. You see how they use their light, and you learn to use yours. There are now two lights shining. You are now able to show others how to let their light shine. The dark room gets brighter as more people enter and start to let their light shine. It is no longer a dark room but a bright glowing place filled with light and positive energy. That's what we can be! That's what we are: "The Light of Positive Power and Energy!"

"In the same way, let your light shine before others, so that they may see your good works and give glory to your Father who is in heaven."
Matthew 5:16 ESV

POSITIVE POWER PRAYER

Dear Lord, I thank you for this day, I thank you for this moment of knowing that I am being thought of in a positive and loving way by others who are reading this at this exact moment. I also thank you for the Power Of The Light, Your Light that shines within and through me. Lord help me to always let my light shine even when I may not feel like it. As my light shines, let it be a beacon that draws others to you. Amen.

Eugenia Johnson-Smith

POSITIVE POWER STUDY

Once you have the light and it is activated, it cannot be hidden. It must shine for all the world to see.

What has caused you to dim or hide your light?

_____
_____
_____
_____
_____

Why is it important for you not to dim or hide your light?

_____
_____
_____
_____
_____
_____
_____
_____
_____
_____
_____

POSITIVE POWER

Now that you have discovered the Power of the Light within you what can you do to help others?

_____
_____
_____
_____

How can you let your light shine to improve your church, school, workplace or community?

_____
_____
_____
_____
_____
_____
_____
_____
_____

How can you help others to discover the light within them?

_____
_____
_____
_____
_____

Eugenia Johnson-Smith

Notes:

POSITIVE POWER

DEVOTION TWENTY-FIVE

The Power of the Present Day

"This is the day that the Lord has made, let us rejoice and be glad in it!"
Psalm 118:24 ESV

Why do we like Fridays better than Mondays? What gave Monday its bad reputation? I have decided that every day is a blessing from God; every day should be treated as a special gift that should be appreciated. I have made it my mission to acknowledge each day with a positive affirmation when I speak, text or email friends, family, and co-workers. It helps to set the tone of the day. Feel free to use them yourself and see how much your attitude for the day and the week improves. Your positive attitude will spread. Go ahead and try one now:

Sunday is Spectacular Sunday or Spiritual Sunday
Monday is Magnificent Monday or Marvelous Monday
Tuesday is Terrific Tuesday
Wednesday is Wonderful Wednesday
Thursday is Thrilling Thursday
Friday is Fabulous Friday or Fantastic Friday
Saturday is Super Saturday

There are no bad days. Every day is a good day. Some days are just better than others. It doesn't matter if it's raining, snowing, or if the sun is shining. They are all good days and we are blessed to have the opportunity to experience each day. He who starts his day seeing the potential of the day has the power to change his life and the power to change the world.

You are in the present day, it is no longer the past. What's done is done. You can't change it. What you can change is your reaction to it. Your acknowledgment, your acceptance, and your ability to leave the past in the past allow every day to be a good day.

> *"If we confess our sins, He is faithful*
> *and just to forgive us our sins and*
> *to cleanse us from all unrighteousness."*
> *1 John 1:9 NKJV*

Did you anger someone? Then apologize. Did you hurt someone? Say you're sorry. Did you steal from someone? Did you take their money, their love, their joy, their dignity, their youth or even their life? What can you do today in the present? What do you want to do?

POSITIVE POWER

Today you have the power to right past wrongs. Don't waste another moment of this day.

An item of note, everyone may not forgive you or accept your apology. But that's okay -- you are not in control of the actions of others. You can only control your own actions. As long as you are sincere in what you say and do, you are doing the right thing. Rest assured, that if you do this, your tomorrow will be better than today because your spirit will be at peace.

You have the power to decide what kind of a day today will be. You have the power to change the way you view each day. Each day is Spectacular, Marvelous, Terrific, Wonderful, Thrilling, Fabulous and Super!

When you need a reminder that God created each day just for you, listen to the song "This Is The Day" by Less Garrett. Crank up the volume and lift up your voice in praise!

Eugenia Johnson-Smith

POSITIVE POWER PRAYER

Dear Lord, I thank you for this day. I thank you for this moment of knowing that I am being thought of in a positive and loving way by others who are reading this at this exact moment. Help me to acknowledge the blessing of the Power of the Present Day no matter what the day. It is a day that is specially made by you and given to me. Help me be grateful for each day I am given. Help me to treat each day as a gift because they are a blessing from you. Amen.

POSITIVE POWER STUDY

Do you value one day more than another?

Which day?

Why?

Who do you need to ask for forgiveness?

Who do you need to forgive?

Eugenia Johnson-Smith

Who do you need to apologize to?

_____
_____
_____
_____
_____

How will you value each new day?

_____
_____
_____
_____
_____

Who do you need to thank?

_____
_____
_____
_____
_____
_____
_____
_____
_____
_____

POSITIVE POWER

Notes:

Eugenia Johnson-Smith

DEVOTION TWENTY-SIX

The Power To Change

Christ is waiting for us to make the change he knows we want to make.

We can change our hair or nails with a quick trip to the barber shop, nail, or hair salon. Some changes we make without much effort. When it is fun and easy we are quick to make the change. But what happens when it is something serious or when it will take time and effort? We are not so quick to make the change in that situation, are we? Even when it's a matter of life and death, we sometimes find it hard to commit to making the change.

We say, "I'm going to change." But when it comes down to it, we can't seem to follow through with the change no matter how important it is to us. We can't seem to do it. We just have to face it. Change is hard and it's hard to change.

If you have tried and failed to make the change on your own, it may be time to seek help. Some things you can only accomplish with God's help. He gives you the strength, courage, and power to make the transformation you seek. Depending on the change you seek there may be support groups you can join. The members of the group can relate to what you're going through. They have been where you are and may have similar experiences to share.

> *"Delight thyself also in the Lord; and he shall give thee the desires of thine heart."*
> *Psalm 37:4 KJV*

With the help of God and others, you have the power to make any change you want. You can be transformed, like a caterpillar to a beautiful butterfly. The change from caterpillar to butterfly occurs in the chrysalis; this is the transition stage of the butterfly's life cycle. The transformation can take a few weeks, months or in some species as long as two years.

However, you must go through the process of breaking through your cocoon in order to have your own personal breakthrough. The length of time it takes for you to complete your transformation shouldn't be compared to that of others. Like the butterfly, your time in your chrysalis is unique to you. The result will be your change or metamorphosis into a new creature. You are no longer the same. *"Therefore if any man be in Christ, he is a new creature; old things are passed away; behold, all things are become new."*

2 Corinthians 5:17 KJV

When confronted by those from your past, those who keep reminding you of who you were before your change, let them know that was the old you. The old you no longer exists. You can boldly declare, "I am no longer that person. That person is gone and will never return."

"Remember ye not the former things, neither consider the things of old."
Isaiah 43:18 KJV

POSITIVE POWER

POSITIVE POWER PRAYER

Dear Lord, I thank you for this day. I thank you for this moment of knowing that I am being thought of in a positive and loving way by others who are reading this at this exact moment. I am thankful for The Power To Change and for your help so that I can let go of the things that are holding me back from living a life that is pleasing to you. I know I need help, and with your help I will make the changes I seek for my life. Amen.

Eugenia Johnson-Smith

POSITIVE POWER STUDY

What changes do you want to make in your life?

_____
_____
_____
_____
_____
_____
_____
_____

Why is it important for you to make these changes?

_____
_____
_____
_____
_____
_____
_____
_____

What will happen if you don't make these changes?

_____
_____

POSITIVE POWER

What will your life be like after your metamorphosis?

Eugenia Johnson-Smith

Notes:

POSITIVE POWER

DEVOTION TWENTY-SEVEN

The Power To Heal

*"Confess your faults one to another, and pray
one for another, that ye may be healed.
The effectual fervent prayer of a
righteous man availeth much."*
James 5:16 KJV

As children we run, we climb on things, we play sports, we fall down and sometimes we get hurt. Cuts, scrapes, and bruises are all a part of life. A kiss from a parent or loved one on the "boo boo," a little salve, a few comforting words, and the healing begins.

Our bodies have the power to heal from injury and sickness. Some healing comes with little or no effort on our part, such as healing from a paper cut. Some healing comes after some discomfort, such as a head cold. Some healing has to come from medication, such as antibiotics. And some healing will only come after a surgical procedure. Each example produces healing in its own time and in its own way.

It is important that we open our hearts, minds and spirits to the power of healing, so we can receive it. When we take time to meditate, pray and visualize, we can send the message of healing to our bodies. This message is received by the subconscious and it is the subconscious that controls the organs of our body. These positive thoughts have the power to heal alone, with or without medical assistance. When healing occurs in this way, it is considered a miracle.

Your healing may come as a result of surgery. Nowadays surgery can be done as an outpatient procedure. You are in and out on the same day. This may give the impression that the surgery is simple, not serious, and you are perfectly normal afterward. That is not necessarily true. The healing process takes time, and your body needs rest to heal. It doesn't matter if the incision is small or the procedure is laparoscopic, it is still surgery and your body must still go through the healing process.

Have you ever prayed for healing and felt that your prayer went unanswered? It is possible that your prayer was answered, just not in the way you anticipated. I recently experienced an illness and I prayed for healing. The healing I was seeking was in the form of a prescription cream, therapy, or both. But that's not the answer I received or expected. Surgery was the answer to my prayer. It was not what I wanted but it was what I needed. Our healing doesn't always come the way we want or expect, but it always comes in the form of what we need.

> *"He healeth the broken in heart,*
> *and bindeth up their wounds."*
> *Psalm 147:3 KJV*

There are times when the healing you seek is not for your physical body but for your mind and your heart. In order for you to heal you may have to remove unhealthy relationships from your life. You may have to cut out an unhealthy lifestyle or even move to a new city or state. You may even need to seek professional help or check into a rehabilitation facility for what you need. Healing that is physical or emotional will not happen overnight. Your body needs time, to heal, to rest, and to process the changes taking place within. It is important that you honor your body and give it the time it needs to heal properly and completely.

Offering forgiveness is part of the healing process when dealing with emotional issues and broken hearts. We need the ultimate healer, God, to heal these wounds. We can find relief in his word and in prayer. Our forgiveness must be given freely with pure intention and without regret even if it is rejected. The act of forgiving is just as important for the giver as it is for the receiver. It is often what starts the healing process and allows us the ability to move forward.

During this process, there may be days of pain, tears, and hard work but you must continue to have a positive mind and spirit. You must see yourself on the other side of your current situation. Keep the faith.

POSITIVE POWER

POSITIVE POWER PRAYER

Dear Lord, I thank you for this day. I thank you for this moment of knowing that I am being thought of in a positive and loving way by others who are reading this at this exact moment. I pray for the healing of my mind, body and spirit. I believe in the Power of Healing and I willingly accept your answer even if it doesn't come as I anticipate. Amen.

Eugenia Johnson-Smith

POSITIVE POWER STUDY

What is your prayer for healing?

_____
_____
_____
_____
_____
_____
_____

How are you preparing your body and mind to receive your healing?

_____
_____
_____
_____

Who can you go to for support?

_____
_____
_____
_____
_____
_____
_____

POSITIVE POWER

List the specific time you will meditate, pray or will engage in positive self talk?

List any previous healing experienced.

Eugenia Johnson-Smith

Notes:

POSITIVE POWER

DEVOTION TWENTY-EIGHT

The Power To Move On

"To every thing there is a season, and a time to every purpose under the heaven: A time to be born, and a time to die; a time to plant, and a time to pluck up that which is planted; A time to kill, and a time to heal; a time to break down, and a time to build up; A time to weep, and a time to laugh; a time to mourn, and a time to dance; A time to cast away stones, and a time to gather stones together; a time to embrace, and a time to refrain from embracing; A time to get, and a time to lose; a time to keep, and a time to cast away; A time to rend, and a time to sew; a time to keep silence, and a time to speak; A time to love, and a time to hate; a time of war, and a time of peace."
Ecclesiastes 3 KJV

Today you may find yourself in a situation in which you feel hopeless or undesirable. Maybe you are in a situation where you can't see your way out.

Be encouraged. This too will pass. Trials, tests, and stumbling blocks that don't kill us or hurt our spirit are meant to make us stronger. These are words we've heard and will continue to hear as we go through life.

When we make it over one hill, we know we can make it over the next. As we climb each hill we become stronger, making the next hill we tackle a bit easier. That's how it is as we face the hills in our lives, and the issues we must move on from.

Life is not a flat or straight line stretching from birth to death. It is an ever-changing undulation of ups and downs, hills and valleys, highs and lows. So if you are currently in your down, valley, or low spot, don't worry because you won't stay there.

Which part of this Bible verse is speaking to you right now? Is it a time to weep? This gives you permission to cry. It's okay to cry. Even Jesus wept.

Remember, when one door closes, another one opens. We just have to be willing to walk through it. Just because we walk in doesn't mean we have to stay there forever. We may only stay for a short while until a window or another door opens.

POSITIVE POWER

"To every thing there is a season, and a time to every purpose under the heaven:"
Ecclesiastes 3:3 KJV

This Bible verse helps us to understand that we will go through changes in our lives and that the situations we will face are not permanent. Your situation will change as the seasons change. You won't always be at the height of happiness but you can always experience Joy, joy in knowing God has a plan for your life and it is to prosper you. So, just as you go through each year, you may experience summer, winter, fall, and spring. You may like one season better than another, but rest assured the season will change after a while, and your favorite one will return just like clockwork.

This current situation may have been a large part of your life and you will have to "mourn" it as a loss in order to move on. And that's okay. In death there is rebirth. The phoenix rises from the ashes and you will, too! It's okay to be in a gloomy or unpleasant situation for a while, but be encouraged, that this too shall pass.

You may feel you are at the end of your rope or "Hope" but you must remember you have resources. There are those in your life who have offered to be there for you in your time of need, be it a listening ear, a shoulder to cry on, or a meal when you are hungry, or a ride to work. Now is the time to take them up on it. You were the caregiver, the helper, the provider, and the one who met the needs of others. When it's your time of need. It's your time to receive. It's your season to be blessed by God through your friends, family, co-workers, or even strangers you don't even know.

I believe God places us on earth to help one another. Today may be your day to receive that help and in the future, it will once again be your day to offer help to someone else.

That's what it means to be a "True Christian" and "Good Samaritan" but you also have to be willing to allow those who love and care for you to offer you their help. Later it will be your season to help sow blessings into others.

Don't cut off those who want to help. If you do, you are interrupting God's Blessings for you and for them as well.

POSITIVE POWER PRAYER

Dear Lord, I thank you for this day. I thank you for this moment of knowing that I am being thought of in a positive and loving way by others who are reading this at this exact moment. Please grant me the Power To Move On and no longer dwell on past situations. Help me to focus my positive power on the here and now. It is here and now that I can make a difference, not in my past. Amen.

Eugenia Johnson-Smith

POSITIVE POWER STUDY

What do you need to move on from?

_____
_____
_____
_____
_____
_____
_____

What steps do you need to take to move on?

_____
_____
_____
_____
_____
_____
_____
_____
_____

What season are you now ready to move into?

_____
_____
_____
_____
_____

POSITIVE POWER

Notes:

Eugenia Johnson-Smith

DEVOTION TWENTY-NINE

The Power To SOAR

"Is it at your command that the eagle mounts up and makes his nest on high? On the cliff he dwells and lodges, Upon the rocky crag, and inaccessibly place. From there he spies out food; His eyes see it from afar."
Job 39:27-29 NASB

What I know and what I believe is that I can do all things through and with Christ, and so can you. We all have that Power within us.

He is my strength when I am weak. He is the wind beneath my wings. He allows me to SOAR like the eagle. And when I SOAR like the Mighty, Magnificent, Majestic Eagle, I am elevated high above all my doubts and fears.

I am higher than my enemies. I am higher than the valleys of doubt and doubters. I can SOAR over the stumbling blocks in my life. I can see far beyond any seemingly hopeless situation I find myself in today.

POSITIVE POWER

Eagles in flight have the ability to see a rabbit from as far as two miles away.

Eagles utilize the updrafts to glide without having to flap their wings. Eagles mate for life; they are committed to their partner.

S Sight Set your sight on looking to the future. Don't let the baggage of your past weigh you down. In order to SOAR you must have a vision. What is your vision for your life? You have to have a clear vision of where you are going so you will know you are on the correct path. You don't want to waste your precious time and energy following the wrong path or missing opportunities.

O Opportunity Be open to all opportunities whether big or small. Take advantage of and use each and every opportunity you are given. Walk through the open doors. You may even have to run to get through the door just before it closes. You might even have to jump out a window or two. Just don't miss your opportunity by not being prepared for it.

A Attitude Attitude is a mindset. If you know you have the power within to be positive, then you will succeed at whatever you do. You may not succeed today but you will reach your goal. Stay inspired and encouraged. Be like the Eagle, be committed to your goals and you will reach them. Look for opportunities, they will not always find you.

R Reach Once you achieve your goal, reach beyond it to your next goal. Each new goal is an opportunity for growth, a chance to spread your wings and SOAR to new heights! Remember you are an EAGLE, not a chicken. You will always seek to reach higher heights. So SOAR!

POSITIVE POWER PRAYER

Dear Lord, I thank you for this day. I thank you for this moment of knowing that I am being thought of in a positive and loving way by others who are reading this at this exact moment. I also thank you for the Power To SOAR! Help me to keep my Sight on the future even when my vision may get blurry. Help me to appreciate All Opportunities you bless me with whether big or small because you don't do anything small. Everything you have planned for my life is for your purpose. Bless me with the Positive Attitude I seek and help me to reach beyond my most lofty Goals. And that by reaching my Goals I will honor, glorify and magnify your name. Amen.

Eugenia Johnson-Smith

POSITIVE POWER STUDY

Sight: I have set my sight on these three short term goals and I will accomplish them within the next six to 12 months.

1)_____
Goal Date:_____

2)_____
Goal Date:_____

3)_____
Goal Date:_____

Opportunity: List three opportunities you are looking for. Note how you are preparing to be ready to walk through the door.

PrepWork:

_____
_____
_____
_____
_____
_____

POSITIVE POWER

Prep Work:

Prep Work:

Attitude: What is the mindset that will keep your spirit lifted on this journey when it gets hard to Soar?

POSITIVE POWER

Reach: I have set my sight on these three long term goals and I will accomplish them within the next three to five years.

_____
Goal Date:_____

_____
Goal Date:_____

_____
Goal Date:_____

Eugenia Johnson-Smith

Notes:

POSITIVE POWER

DEVOTION THIRTY

The Power To Succeed

*"Commit your actions to the LORD,
and your plans will succeed."*
Proverbs 16:3 NLT

You are not a failure! We were born with everything we need to succeed. That being said, we should never view ourselves as failures. Sure, we may fail to achieve our desired outcome, or get the degree of success we intended; however, there were bits of success in the outcome.

Don't sell yourself short. Every now and then we all fall short or fail to hit that high goal we set. But that in no way makes us failures. We are not defined by our failures. We are made stronger by them, and our character is shaped by them. Our character is determined by how we deal with and react to those specific failures in our lives. We may call them stumbling blocks, trials, and tribulations, or maybe "what was I thinking?" moments.

Have you heard the song, "We fall down," by Donnie McClurkin? The key message in his song is getting up. Picking yourself up, dusting yourself off, straightening your tie, adjusting your skirt, fluffing your hair, moving on, and shaking it off. Act like a duck, let the water roll off your back. No matter how many times you fall down, you get back up. You don't stay down.

How many of you would consider Oprah Winfrey, Beyonce`, Tyler Perry, Michael Jordan, Henry Ford, Walt Disney, or Milton S. Hershey a failure? I bet most of you wouldn't consider them to be failures. However, prior to their success, they had a few failures. Yet that didn't stop them from pursuing their dreams of success. Now if they had let those specific failures stop them, they would never have become the multimillionaires they are today.

These individuals faced and overcame stumbling blocks or challenges in their lifetimes. We too are faced with our own set of challenges to overcome. We need to focus on how we are going to overcome them. Once we determine our plan, we are better able to focus on meeting the challenge. Once we view the challenges as temporary and not permanent, we are better able to tackle them.

You will be faced with a number of challenges throughout your life. Many of them may come from your family and friends in the form of negative talk, "You are wasting your time," "You're throwing your money away," or "I told you it wouldn't work or it was a bad idea anyway."

We don't plan to fail; that's why we take it so hard when we don't reach our expected goal. Especially if we are overachievers and if everything has come easy before.

We sometimes simply fail to plan. We don't put time into the preparation needed to get the expected outcome. Or maybe we don't anticipate potential challenges or obstacles that may come up.

What does your SUCCESS look like? Only you can answer that question. You will only have a clear vision of your success when you have prayed on it and can answer that question truthfully.

Everyone's vision of success is different. We need not compare our success to that of others. Your vision may not be to own a mansion with 16 bedrooms, 7 bathrooms, and a five-car garage but rather own a home that meets your needs.

Is your goal to further your education by finishing high school, college or earning your GED? Is your goal to get all of your children through college, out of your house, and independent? Is your goal retirement with financial stability? Is this what success looks like to you?

Or maybe your idea of SUCCESS is getting through the day without giving in to a past addiction.

Or maybe your idea of SUCCESS is finally getting up the nerve to leave a relationship that has been abusive or toxic or that has killed the spirit of your joy or of who you are.

We are the author of the book of our lives and we can write and rewrite; add and delete; edit and revise it at any time and as many times as

POSITIVE POWER

we want. As a reminder, this is your vision of your success and not that of your mother, father, children, significant other, or best friend. Only you can define what it means for you to succeed.

Eugenia Johnson-Smith

POSITIVE POWER PRAYER

Dear Lord, I thank you for this day. I thank you for this moment of knowing that I am being thought of in a positive and loving way by others who are reading this at this exact moment. I also thank you for the Power To Succeed! I ask guidance over my life as I seek a vision of my success for me as you have ordained. Amen.

POSITIVE POWER STUDY

What are some of the challenges you've had to overcome?

_____
_____
_____
_____
_____
_____
_____
_____

How did you deal with a past failure?

_____
_____
_____
_____
_____
_____
_____
_____
_____
_____

Write your vision for success.

Outline the steps you will take in order for you to succeed.

POSITIVE POWER

Notes:

Eugenia Johnson-Smith

DEVOTION THIRTY-ONE

The Power To Witness

"But ye shall receive power, after that the Holy Ghost is come upon you; and ye shall be witnesses unto me both in Jerusalem, and in all Judaea, and in Samaria, and unto the uttermost parts of the earth."
Acts 1:8 KJV

W Willing

I Individuals

T Telling

N Neighbors

E Everything the

S Savior

S Said or did for you

The Bible instructs us to tell the good news. Sharing it helps us as well as others. When we

POSITIVE POWER

tell our stories of what God has brought us through, it gives us strength to get through the next storm or situation that may come our way. It lets us know that the problems or issues we thought were so big or bad in our eyes were not so big or bad for God.

When others hear what we've gone through with God's help, seemingly impossible or hopeless situations, they will know they can make it, too. The key is that we did not do it on our own. We had God's help.

It's giving credit for a job well done. God got us through the situation. It wasn't us so we shouldn't take the credit. We have to let everyone know who did "the heavy lifting." That is what witnessing is: telling or sharing what God has done for you, what he has done for your family, and what he has done for others. Your witnessing will encourage others by letting them know that they, too, can call on God to help deal with any situation they may face in life. It may touch the hearts of others by giving them the courage to be a witness to what God has done for them in their lives.

Eugenia Johnson-Smith

"For God hath not given us the spirit of fear, but of power, and of love, and of a sound mind."
2 Timothy 1:7 KJV

We should not be afraid to stand up and tell at least one thing God has done for us. For he has done far more than one thing for each of us. If we stop and think about it. I'm sure we don't have enough fingers and toes to count all the blessings he has given us today. We don't have to use fancy words, we just need to be willing to let others know that God is in control of our lives.

Even a child can witness. He is the one who provides food, and shelter for me. He gives me a mommy and a daddy to love. He takes care of my sisters, brothers and friends.

POSITIVE POWER PRAYER

Dear Lord, I thank you for this day. I thank you for this moment of knowing that I am being thought of in a positive and loving way by others who are reading this at this exact moment. Thank you for the Power To Witness. I thank you for all you have done for me and I am willing to share it with others. I know that my sharing will help others. Amen.

Eugenia Johnson-Smith

POSITIVE POWER STUDY

How do you share what God has done for you?

Why do you share?

POSITIVE POWER

How do you encourage others to share what God has done for them?

___

What is your reason(s) for not sharing if you don't currently share what God has done for you?

___

Eugenia Johnson-Smith

Share your testimony. What has God done for you?

POSITIVE POWER

Notes:

Eugenia Johnson-Smith

MY POSITIVE POWER PRAYER FOR YOU

This is more than a book, it's my gift to you. This devotion has been prayed over, anointed, and given to God. It's my witness of what God has done for me and who He is in my life. It's me letting my light shine through my words on these pages.

As you read, meditated, and communed with God you may have opened your heart and soul up for the first time. Some of the devotions may have been hard for you and you may still have work to do to fully unleash your Positive Power. That is okay, everyone is on their own journey. They alone will know when they have reached their destination. As I said in the Power of Direction, you can rest, change directions, or start all over again. You may revisit one or all the devotions at any time depending on your current situation. Each devotion will touch your heart in the way you need it as you read it.

I pray that it has touched your heart, soul, and mind and allowed you to unleash your Positive Power. Having Positive Power will not prevent

POSITIVE POWER

you from having bad and unpleasant experiences. But it will help you meet and overcome them with a positive spirit.

You can let your light shine without fear. You are not alone, you are now part of Positive Power People, P3. I pray that you believe you can do all things with Christ and choose to live a Positive Power life of forgiveness, hope, and salvation.

Yours in Christ,

Eugenia